G000123933

# Who Are You?

**On the evolutionary path that
can lead to transhumanism or
created in the image of God?**

## B M COAKER

authorHOUSE®

*AuthorHouse™ UK*
*1663 Liberty Drive*
*Bloomington, IN 47403 USA*
*www.authorhouse.co.uk*
*Phone: 0800.197.4150*

*Scripture quotations marked KJV are from the Holy Bible, King James Version (Authorized Version). First published in 1611. Quoted from the KJV Classic Reference Bible, Copyright © 1983 by The Zondervan Corporation.*

*Copyright request, Scripture quotations are taken from the King James Easy Read Bible, KJVER, ©2001, 2007, 2010, 2015 by Whitaker House.*

*Unless otherwise indicated, all Scripture quotations are taken from the King James Easy Read Bible, KJVER©2001, 2007, 2010, 2015 by Whitaker House. Used by permission. All rights reserved.*

*Published by AuthorHouse  02/27/2018*

*ISBN: 978-1-5462-8902-9 (sc)*
*ISBN: 978-1-5462-8901-2 (e)*

*Print information available on the last page.*

*Any people depicted in stock imagery provided by Getty Images are models, and such images are being used for illustrative purposes only. Certain stock imagery © Getty Images.*

*This book is printed on acid-free paper.*

# CONTENTS

Dedicated to my five grandchildren, in the hope that they follow Christ unswervingly throughout their lives and that they believe in the inerrant Word of Almighty God:

Tobias Paul Williams
Grace Hope Williams
Joseph Abraham Williams
Daniel Evan Coaker
Abby Rose Coaker

# ACKNOWLEDGEMENTS

My grateful thanks go to Linda Rieder, Robert Greaves, and Pastor Simon Lawrenson for their advice, comments, and critique of the manuscript as it progressed.

Also thanks to Pastor Barry Forder and David Rossevear (CSM), who read and commented on the manuscript; Mathew Thompson, who used his IT skills to prepare the book for submission; and Hilary Thompson, who has been my prayer companion from beginning to end and has offered constant support and encouragement.

# INTRODUCTION

What is it that makes a human being human? Did we evolve or were we created? The answers to these questions are important when considering the implications of transhumanism.

*WhoAreYou?* is an intentionally small book that considers these questions. Through the pages, Christians are encouraged to address the subject of transhumanism from the foundation of the inerrant and living Word of God. How we perceive the person of Jesus Christ has a profound effect on how we perceive ourselves and the many issues surrounding the prospect of transhumanism. The creationist worldview and the evolutionist worldview play an important part in how you may view transhumanism.

This book has been designed to offer a starting point on your path of discovery. Perhaps at the end you will know who you are, and who you are not, and who you do not need to be.

# CHAPTER 1

## The Starting Point (Along the Evolutionary Path)

You are worthy o Lord, to receive glory and
honor and power; for You have created all
things, and for Your pleasure they are and
were created.

—Revelation 4:11

Life is challenging! It rushes relentlessly forward over the
rough and smooth terrain of our circumstances but never
stays still. Our thoughts and ideas keep forging ahead to
keep pace with the society in which we live. Sometimes we
need to make ourselves stop. We need to pause and reflect.
Who am I? Who are you? Where does it all begin? We will
start with the evolutionary path.

The theory of evolution has its own starting point: the
belief that naturally occurring, chance processes advance
through trial and error over millions of years. The process

of evolution is loosely based on the criteria of microevolution and macroevolution. *Microevolution* refers to small adaptive changes within a species. Microevolution is acknowledged by proponents of creation because it is supported by observable science, but only within a species. *Macroevolution* refers to one kind changing into another kind, which has not been supported by observable science. Generally speaking, evolutionists refer to this as "transitional" fossils or "missing links" when they talk of the "evolutionary tree".

Advocates of evolution (i.e., atheists and agnostics) find it hard to believe in any divine intervention or even the existence of God. Some may broadly accept the following evolution model of origins:

- Over billions of years, the universe, the solar system, the earth, and finally life developed from disordered matter through natural processes.
- Random mutations and natural selection brought about all life from single-celled life.
- All life has a common ancestor.[1]

The theory of evolution is constantly changing as new information arises, but the bottom line only accepts the origin of life from natural processes. Such is the basis for the worldview of atheism—to explain all things without God. For other proponents, the evolutionary starting point would likely include a nature god or a multitude of gods, such as the worldviews of paganism, pantheism, and animism.

---

[1] W. Brown, *In the Beginning*: Compelling Evidence for Creation and the Flood, 8th edn
(Phoenix, AZ: Center for Scientific Creation 2008), 397.

The type of evolution that is more popularly believed by transhumanists is macroevolution, which opens the door to 'assisting mankind' to reach the next stage of evolution and become a so-called 'higher species.' This is inconsistent with scripture, which states that every creature was created 'after its kind' (Gen.1:21, 24–25.) This is emphasized: 'All flesh is not the same flesh; but there is one kind of flesh of men, another flesh of beasts, another of fishes, and another of birds' (1Cor.15:39).

From a biblical perspective, this God-given information makes it impossible to reconcile the evolutionary belief that humankind has animal ancestry or that millions of years ago, birds, for instance, evolved from dinosaurs.

Creationists have a much less flexible belief system, based on the foundation of Holy Scripture. They accept the following criteria, the creation model of origins:

- Everything in the universe, including the stars, the solar system, the earth, life, and humans, came into existence suddenly and recently, with essentially the complexity
- We see today.
- Genetic variations are limited.
- The earth has experienced a worldwide flood.[2]

For the Christian, the starting point has to be Jesus, Son of God and Son of Man. Our relationship to Him, or our lack of relationship to Him, is the pivotal point of everything we think, say, do, and believe. He is the embodiment of the inerrant Word of God: 'In the beginning was the Word, and the Word was with God, and the Word was God. The

---

[2] Ibid.

same was in the beginning with God. All things were made by Him; and without Him was not anything made that was made' (John 1:1–3).

Partial belief in scripture can only lead us to dangerous ground. It should be acknowledged as all truth or no truth, never partial truth. Ask yourself this question. What is the Word of God? Is it birthed in holiness, perfect wisdom, in absolute power and authority? What absolute could possibly be higher than that? Certainly not the restless and ever changing word of man. There is no better basis for the foundation of life than the inerrant Word of God.

Sadly, we all get it wrong sometimes, and this tends to lead us to grey areas where our own thoughts and doubts override the perfect truth of God's Word. This can lead us towards a secular and humanistic approach to scripture, which can take us in a different direction from that which scripture teaches us to follow.

As life marches on, knowledge from our peers is built upon, and we gain from their experience. However, as knowledge improves, sometimes we find that previous knowledge wasn't correct. People had to work within smaller parameters that didn't clarify the depth of information that is accessible to us now—knowledge that was simply not possible for generations to learn in the past.

Darwinism is one example of this. If Darwin had had access to the more advanced sciences we have today, would he have continued to believe in evolution? Would he have written his famous book *On the Origin of Species*? When we take into account the huge advances in technology, which have supposedly opened doors that were unheard of just a couple of decades ago, we can appreciate that it is easier now to acquire information and utilize it than it was for our predecessors.

Because of this, it becomes necessary sometimes to re-evaluate what we have learned in the past, to see if some things have changed.

Although God's Word never changes, humankind's word is constantly changing, and so too is our perception of the world around us. Ideally *creation* and *evolution* are not words that we should use interchangeably, as they are not compatible. Yet at times, Christians marry the two words in the term *theistic evolution*. One consequence of this is that the weed of doubt has already raised its head and called into question the authenticity of scripture—that is, God's character, power, and authority. 'Did He really say?' 'Did He really do?'

For the Christian, it is better not to walk on this path. It is best to choose the route of creationism and use God's Word as an anchor. We can measure our understanding of any given subject in relation to His Word. This acknowledges His divine authority.

When this is not done, we foster an inaccurate understanding of our Triune God: the person of God the Father, the person of God the Son, and the person of God the Holy Spirit. We also misunderstand the information that scripture gives us. We deviate from the pure and holy way and instead choose to follow a different path of our own making, such as the one that begins with the theory of evolution.

Sadly, instead of standing solidly on the foundation of God's Word, many have chosen instead to stand on their own knowledge. This is not a very stable foundation, as many have found out in the past and will continue to do in the future. Among the proponent of evolution, theories of human origins are constantly changing and being discarded. This only leads to a path away from Christ instead of towards Him. On the subject of evolution, there is bound to be conflict because God's own account of creation is in question.[3]

In young earth creationism, God's account is taken literally in terms of the timeframe of six days times twenty-four hours, plus twenty-four hours of rest. This corresponds to our calendar week and to the twenty-four-hour rotation of the earth. As mentioned, the path of evolution deviates from this, by embracing a different timeframe that accommodates the naturalistic belief of evolution over millions of years rather than the biblical account. This is the dilemma faced by Christians who believe in the theory of evolution. Please read the following account:

> Many people, although they may not know the term, are theistic evolutionists; that is, they believe God used evolution to create the universe and everything in it. For some, this is an acceptable compromise-belief in at least some aspects of evolution and belief in God. The first provides scientific respectability, while the second satisfies an inward conviction that there must be a Creator. For these people, evolution is

---

[3] To look at the subject of young earth creation in detail, a very good book to read is *Faith, Form, and Time* by Kurt P. Wise. Of particular interest is chapter 4, entitled 'How Old Are Things?'

compatible with the Bible. But is it? Since Darwin's time (mid-late 1800s), many who knew what the Bible said have tried to reinterpret scripture to make it compatible with the theory of evolution. The fact that there are about twenty theistic evolution theories indicates the general dissatisfaction with each. It also suggests that reconciling evolution with the Bible is not as easy as some claim.[4]

This does not affect the act of salvation in any way, but it appears to make scripture a less than perfect authority. Doubt leads to more doubt, which can eventually lead to disbelief. The different time span itself is not the overriding issue, although some people would disagree on this point. The main issue is to do with the Sovereign authority of scripture.

The theory of evolution denies the supernatural creation of humanity and the spiritual aspect that was part of humanity's creation in the image of God. 'And so it is written. The first man Adam was made a living soul; the last Adam was made a quickening spirit' (1 Cor.15:45). Instead, the theory of evolution favours the belief of mammalian descent, and does not recognize the intimacy of God in the human race. This is the path that can lead a person who has some Christian belief in the opposite direction from God's Word.

---

[4] W. Brown, *In the Beginning*: Compelling Evidence for Creation and the Flood, 8th edn. (Phoenix, AZ: Centre for Scientific Creation, 2008), 387

Some people mistakenly believe that science and Christianity do not mix. The term *science* is a blanket that covers many fields of inquiry. The theory of evolution is often mistakenly considered a similar blanket. It is, in fact, origins science, (sometimes referred to as forensic science), and unobservable. Observable science can be tested. There are many Christian scientists who are experts in fields of observable science. For instance, the famous astronomer Johannes Keplar is well known for the expression "to think God's thoughts after him". Their scientific pursuits give them heightened awareness of the amazing attributes of God. In another example, Mathew Fontaine Maury (1806-1873), is often esteemed in the arena of scientific endeavour for being the "father of oceanography" His research was apparently based on Psalm 8:8 that informs us of "the paths of the sea". He was a firm believer in the trustworthiness of Scripture. He believed that there were paths in the sea, and he decided to look for them. Consequently he discovered the ocean currents.

There are other seeds of truth within scripture. Job 26:7 states "he hangs the earth upon nothing". 1 Corinthians 15:41 speaks of the different qualities of the sun, moon and stars. Since the quality and precision of telescopes has improved over the years, it is widely known that the stars are different in components and structure. Likewise, the words of Jeremiah 33:22 are now known to be true. Neither the stars, nor sand can be measured. Stars range in the billions, as does the grains of sand found on the seashore.

In his excellent little book "Scientific Facts of the Bible", R Comfort draws our attention to the statement of Arthur H Compton, a Nobel Prize winner in Physics. He looked at the design of Creation and came to the conclusion that an orderly universe points to God and intelligent design (see recommended reading).

Some scientists who base their work on the world view of evolution also find it difficult not to question their own world view on origins. For instance, the gaps in the fossil record, the missing links that are still missing, the loss of information in DNA mutations and the lack of evidence for any gain of information all prove frustrating for the proponents of evolution, and is causing ever widening holes in the fabric of their expectations of the progression of the evolutionary path. Science does not appear to consistently support the theory of evolution. Therefore the hopes and dreams concerning transhumanism already appear to have a shaky foundation.

Some followers of transhumanism within the theistic evolution camp believe that it is the way forward to live forever, to advance the perceived progression of evolution. That is contrary to Scripture in every sense.

If we perform even a quick scrutiny of biblical implications regarding the theory of evolution, we could ask ourselves this: if there were death and destruction before Adam and Eve, then why would death be the judgement for sin?

Sin could not have existed before the Fall, as God had pronounced the finished act of creation 'very good' (Gen.1:31).

Adam was created from the dust of the earth (Gen.2:7). But if the earth had been contaminated with the remains of dead things, then Adam would not have been perfectly formed from the dust of the earth. He could not have been deemed 'very good'. God is holy and cannot lie, so surely any assumption of death before sin is incorrect.

Let's take a step further along the path that began with the belief in evolutionary origins to take a closer look at transhumanism. What is transhumanism? Take a look online or in bookstores and you may realise that the concept of transhumanism has been with us for some time, and that most Governments throughout the world are investing billions into furthering its progress through advanced technology. It stems from the popular belief of 'helping evolution' to transform humanity to a higher level of existence. This would be for the purpose of overcoming our physical limitations.

Once this current worldly belief system becomes merged with God's inerrant version of origins, the Christian worldview will change. The ground is prepared to embrace the aspirations of transhumanism. The theistic evolutionists have a problem and will need to evaluate their own beliefs accordingly.

It is generally accepted that the main push towards transhumanism is intended to form a new higher species through adaption to modern technology. It is believed that the use of genetic engineering will play a large part towards this achievement. Genetic research and experimentation is advancing in leaps and bounds. Although this may prove invaluable to the health industry, it appears to be striding a long way beyond that ideal, to "re-invent" God given humanity to man's ideal of "supermen" in man's image.

This is not to say that all technological advancement will go this way. The invention and use of technology has always been an integral part of who we are. God is Creator and has given us the ability to make things using substances that He has already provided for us. So technology, as such, has His seal of authority. He has not given us the authority to create humans in His image. To attempt to do so is likely to incur His wrath rather than His blessing.

Technology has always been utilized by man:

> And Adam knew Eve his wife; and she conceived, and bare Cain, and said, I have gotten a man from the Lord. And she again bare his brother Abel. And Abel was a keeper of sheep, but Cain was a tiller of the ground. (Gen.4:1–2)

> And Cain knew his wife; and she conceived, and bare Enoch: and he builder a city, and called the name of the city, after the name of his son, Enoch. (Gen.4:17)

> And Adah bare Ja-bal: he was the father of such as dwell in tents, and of such as have cattle. And his brother's name was Ju-bal: he was the father of all such as handle the harp and organ. And Zil-ah, she also bare Tu-balcain, an instructor of every artificer in brass and iron. (Gen.4:20–22)

We can see that the first humans were skilled in many ways. They developed the means for agriculture, farming, tent making, construction, instrument making, and the manufacturing of metals. By the time of the worldwide Flood, a chronological timeline of 1,656 years, they were able to invent and make things with great precision and accuracy.

Following the blueprint given to Noah by God, the ark was constructed using gopher wood(Gen. 6:14–16). Gopher wood is now more commonly known as cypress, and the island of Cyprus is named after its abundance of this wood. Noah and his family had the ability to fell trees and cut them up to God's required width, length, and thickness. Not only that, they had to fit everything together precisely as well, because the ark had to endure unprecedented pressure, probably greater than the pressures upon ocean vessels of current times. The ark survived everything that occurred during the Flood, and brought its occupants safely to rest. It is unlikely that sea-going vessels of today would remain unscathed given the same conditions that the ark endured. Therefore the assumption can be made that technology in those early days was of a high standard.

After the Flood, technology was still in play. Cities, weapons, and tools were made. Archaeologists are still making many discoveries attesting to the sophistication of early civilizations.

You may be surprised to know that in the year 1900, a sunken ship was discovered in the Aegean Sea. It was dated as BC (that is Before Christ). An object was discovered on the sunken vessel, and painstakingly uncovered to reveal a mechanism that was named the "Antikythera". Inside this container were constructed more than thirty high quality bronze gears of high complexity. It was studied by a man called Derek de Solla Price, who made a working model of the device. He concluded that its purpose was to compute solar and lunar cycles. It was an early analog computing device. Price showed that it was a planetarium for the motions of the sun and moon.[5]

It appears that human beings were intelligent and had numerous abilities to fashion the world in which they lived. So where did everything go wrong? We have to go back to the very beginning, to Satan's legacy.

---

[5] D. E. Chittick, *The Puzzle of Ancient Man: Evidence for Advanced Technology in Past Civilizations*, 3rd edn. (Newburg, Oregon: Creation Compass, 2006), 9.

# CHAPTER 2

## Satan's Legacy

Again, the devil takes Him up into an exceeding high mountain, and shows Him all the kingdoms of the world, and the glory of them; And says to Him, All these things will I give you, if You will fall down and worship me. Then says Jesus to him, Get you from here, Satan; for it is written, You shall worship the Lord your God, and Him only will you serve.

—Matthew 4:8–10

Why do so many people turn away from God's truth to believe a lie? How does this lead to transhumanism? The Bible verse quoted above may hold part of the answer.

In this encounter with Jesus, Satan obviously chose to ignore the fact that he was addressing the Creator of the heavens and the earth. He offered Jesus what already belonged to Jesus. Satan did not have ownership of the heavens and the earth, but in this instance, he assumed it. He offers the heavens and the earth to Jesus in Jesus' humanity as Son of Man, rather than as Son of God.

The temptation offered to Jesus was the same lie that Satan offers us. That is, Satan offers falsely assumed power and authority in return for us following Satan in his rebellion against God. We have an irrevocable choice: to follow the precepts of our Triune God or those of Satan, the rebel and usurper.

As we look at our world today, we can see the evidence of this desire for power and control. War, murder, and other violence occur in the pursuit of power. We can even see it to a lesser extent in family life, in arguments and disagreements. We see it in work situations, in rivalry, and among those climbing the ladder of success.

We are all prone to this temptation without even thinking about its origin. However, when we become aware of it, we realize that Jesus has shown us how to counter-attack by using the Word of God:

> Stand therefore, having your loins girt about with truth, and having on the breastplate of righteousness; And your feet shod with the preparation of the Gospel of peace; Above all, taking the shield of faith, wherewith you shall be able to quench all the fiery darts of the wicked. And take the helmet of Salvation, and the sword of the Spirit, which is the Word of God. (Eph.6:14–17)

When Satan says 'I will give you,' we should be on our guard. And our reply should begin, 'It is written'.

This same principle now at work in us is currently manifesting itself through the ideals of transhumanism. Transhumanism also says 'I will give you'. However, there is a fatal price to pay. Satan demands worship of himself in return. The pursuit of transhumanism should be studied in light of what God's Word says, because the Word is a guiding principle for every aspect of the human experience. We have an unseen enemy: 'Be sober, be vigilant; because your adversary the devil, as a roaring lion, walks about, seeking whom he may devour' (1 Pet.5:8).

As we don't see the wind, only the effects of it, we don't see the attacks of Satan but we do see the results.

How did this happen? How will this pan out?

Satan is a created, angelic being: 'All things were made through Him [Jesus], and without Him was not anything made that was made' (John 1:3). Satan was created before human beings, as one of a host of witnesses to God's creation of the earth. This is revealed through scripture when God questions Job, a prophet of the Old Testament. God said, when questioning Job:

> Where were you when I laid the foundations of the earth? declare, if you have understanding.
>
> Who has laid the measures thereof, if you know? or who has stretched the line upon it?
>
> Whereupon are the foundations thereof fastened? or who laid the cornerstone thereof;

When the morning stars sang together and
all the sons of God shouted for joy? (Job
38:4–7)

Satan, also known as Lucifer, was originally the covering
cherub of the order of cherubim. He covered the mercy seat
and walked among the coals, the holy fire of God:

You are the anointed cherub that covers; and I have
set you so; you were upon the holy mountain of God; you
have walked up and down in the midst of the stones of fire.
(Ezek.28:14).

The cherubim are holy angels who are proximate to
God on His throne. They are associated with the lifting
up and transporting of His glory (see Ezek.10).Lucifer
was originally described as perfect, as befitted a divinely
created being, before he rebelled against God. He was full
of wisdom and perfect in beauty, with coverings of jewels
prepared for him on the day of his creation (Ezek.28:13–15).
It was perhaps (this is conjecture) his privilege to oversee the
very first human beings created in the image of God, who
were placed in the Garden of Eden. His role at that time,
perhaps, to minister to them:

Are they not all ministering spirits, sent forth to minister
for them who shall be heirs of Salvation? (Heb.1:14).

Ministering would have involved leaving heaven to go
to earth—moving from the spiritual realm to the physical
realm. There are many references in the Bible to times when
angels have taken human form in order to fulfil the will of
God (see Gen. 18; Dan. 8:15–17; Heb. 13:2).

It was in the Garden of Eden that everything went wrong for humanity. The first man, Adam, had been formed by God and then placed in the Garden:

And the Lord God formed man of the dust of the ground, and breathed into his nostrils the breath of life; and man became a living soul. And the Lord God planted a garden eastward in Eden; and there He put the Man whom He had formed' (Gen.2:7–8).[1]

Eve was created as the first woman out of the side of Adam (Gen. 2:21–22). This was to continue the line of 'one flesh' right from the beginning—an important fact. This was the pattern for the perpetuation of the human race:

And Adam said, This is now bone of my bones, and flesh of my flesh: she shall be called Woman, because she was taken out of Man. Therefore shall a man leave his father and his mother, and shall cling to his wife: and they shall be one flesh. (Gen.2:23–24).

---

[1] It is humbling to note that this was Jesus, who is the Lord God. For those of us who are Christians, Jesus has given us life twice: first through creation, then again through salvation. We are truly born again in every sense.

It is also interesting to note that by the Lord's breathing into the nostrils, confirmation is given to us that our 'breath of life' is totally different from the life given to the animal kingdom. Their 'breath of life' was given in a different manner. Right from the start, this attributed more value to the man than to the angels. There is no record of God having breathed life into angels who are, after all, Spirits. We may assume that angels were created through God's Word: 'You, even You, are Lord alone; You have made heaven, the heaven of heavens, with all their host, the earth, and all things that are therein, the seas, and all that is therein, and You preserve them all; and the host of heaven worship you' (Neh. 9:6).

The holy angels are a totally different creation of God, although generally referred to in the context of "male" throughout Scripture. As totally distinct from mankind, it follows that angels would not have been permitted to cohabitate with human women. (This is exactly what some of the fallen angels actually did, resulting in the hybrid nephilim. This was a strategy to corrupt the status of mankind in the image of God. This is an interesting point because our society and transhumanism appears to be currently taking steps towards a similar scenario. Another attempt to corrupt mankind created in the image of God. (More on this later.)

To witness the creation of woman, therefore, was a momentous event, as well as the creation of man. It was an incredible act of creation in a very personal way.

It does not seem improbable that Lucifer, as the anointed and covering cherub, was among the angelic host that sang and shouted for joy as they witnessed God's handiwork of creation. Bible references to angels show that one of their roles is to worship God, and surely this would include praise and worship for His act of creation.

Again, this is purely my conjecture, but perhaps the 'light bearer' assumed that the entire act of creation was for the angels. After all, at that point, they were the only beings that God had made. When Adam and Eve were formed personally by God and in His image, perhaps Lucifer became aware that God's plan was different to his own expectations.

Dominion of the earth was given to humanity:

And God blessed them, and God said to them, Be fruitful and multiply, and replenish the earth, and subdue it: and have dominion over the fish of the sea, and over the fowl of the air, and over every living thing that moves upon the earth (Gen.1:28).

Lucifer would have been aware that God's will was the highest authority, and that he was expected to be subject to it. Rather than humanity being under his authority in turn, these two people were the beginning of a special race, created to have a special relationship with God. Human beings were under God's blessing and authority, rather than under Lucifer's own presumed power and authority.

Angels were created to worship God in heaven, and the human race was created to worship God on earth. Lucifer wanted that worship for himself, but God's Word is very specific: My Glory I will not give to another (Isa.42:8).

The name Satan means 'adversary' in the Hebrew language, the original language in which the Old Testament was written. The moment that sin entered into him in the form of pride, he became opposed to God and everything God stood for. Satan would no longer willingly submit to God's authority. He rejected the Godhead in favour of pursuing his own will. His intention was to be his own god. His plan was to take mankind for his own purposes, and to be their ruling authority and the subject of their worship.

Satan began his plan by casting doubt on the Word of God. This is something he continues to do. He takes a grain of truth from God's Word and twists it to take away its meaning and value. He could not force Eve to sin, so he tempted her and deceived her to submit to his will, in defiance of God's will.

And so the human race fell into sin, guided by Satan, as willing participants. Since the events in the Garden of Eden, this warfare has continued. It now moves towards its climax, as transhumanism inevitably draws us closer to the point of no return, where humanity falls beneath the lies and deceit of Satan.

In God's written Word, Satan has many names. Let's look at some of them to get a clearer picture of the character of our enemy:

- Devil (diabolos) or 'false accuser' (Zech.3:1)
- Slanderer (Job 1:2)
- Tempter (1 Thess.3:5)
- Beelzebub (Matt.12:24)
- Originator of sin (1 John 3:8)
- Accuser (Rev.12:10)
- Wicked one (Matt.13:19)
- Ruler of this world (John 12:31)
- God of this age (2 Cor.4:4)
- Dragon (Rev.12:9)
- Angel of light (2 Cor.11:14)
- Ruler of demons (Matt.12:24)
- Abaddon or 'destroying angel'(Rev.9:11)
- Antichrist (1 John 4:3)
- Crooked serpent (Isa.27:1)
- Thief/stealer (John 10:9)

What do these names tell us? Satan is constantly reminding us of our sinful condition, although he himself was the instigator of it. He does not tell us that there is a way out'. He is always trying to persuade us that God is less than God says He is. Not least, Satan tells us that evolution made the world and everything in it, when the Bible teaches otherwise. He is the false accuser who tells us that we're not good enough to be saved. God's Word is explicit to the contrary: Verily, verily, I say to you, He that hears My word, and believes on Him that sent Me, has everlasting life, and shall not come into condemnation; but is passed from death to life (John 5:24).

Satan constantly tempts us into living independently of God, to live only to for self and self-motivation. He is the ruler of this world. We are born under his rule. Thankfully, we do not have to stay under his rule. We are his servants by default. If we do nothing, we belong in his kingdom. If we choose to live by faith in Jesus Christ, we change our ruling authority to Christ. We belong to Satan's kingdom unless we choose Christ's kingdom.

Satan is the originator of sin. He is the originator of all that is wrong with the world. So many times, we blame God for the atrocities in the world instead of laying the blame at Satan's feet and our own, for it is our desires that lead to sin: But every man is tempted, when he is drawn away of his own lust, and enticed. Then when lust has conceived, it brings forth sin; and sin, when it is finished, brings forth death (Jas. 1:14–15).

It is so sad that some people have more faith in what technology can do for us than in what Christ has already done for us. Christ is the only way forward to eternity. Satan deceives us. As an 'angel of light', he blinds us so that we perceive bad as good. Like the fruit in the Garden of Eden, he shows us things that look good on the outside, and desirable, when in reality they can be destructive. In our fallen condition, we cannot recognize his evil intentions.

Take technology. What a difference it has made in our lives to have a mobile phone, and then an iPad, and then apps. These tools make daily routines much quicker and communication much faster. They have transformed our society.

But we're never satisfied. We want more and more. So now we are ruled by technology, increasingly subservient to and reliant upon it. For instance, it is hard to get a job without first putting your CV online. That is fast becoming a basic necessity for those seeking employment. That may seem natural to this generation, but not so much for their grandparents.

Before long, we may not have paper money. It could well become digital money. This would be great for some, but restrictive for those who don't want a cashless society. Perhaps elderly people would not know how to live in that kind of society.

We are prone to be never satisfied with what we have. That is the lure of Satan, and we should proceed with caution.

> Be sober, be vigilant; because your adversary the devil, as a roaring lion, walks about, seeking whom he may devour.(1 Pet.5:8)

> And the Lord said to Satan, From where come you? Then Satan answered the Lord, and said, From going to and fro in the earth, and from walking up and down in it (Job 1:7).

> Jesus said to his accusers: You are of your father the devil, and the lusts of your father you will do. He was a murderer from the beginning, and abode not in the truth, because there is no truth in him. When he speaks a lie, he speaks of his own; for he is a liar and the father of it (John 8:44).

We see here the progressively dangerous path that deviating from the Word of God will take us. None of us are perfect. Each one of us has deviated from this path at some point, probably many times. But God's Word and will ensure that we can turn back if we are willing to turn to Christ. We do not have to walk on Satan's path to everlasting destruction.

Look how far Satan has fallen. The list of names accorded to him is long, and none of them are good or complimentary. Satan no longer shines with the holy fire of the Presence of God. He no longer has authority as the covering cherub. But his aspirations remain high, and he is still ambitious to wrest the kingdom of God for himself, using mankind as his pawns.

Thankfully, Satan's power over us was broken by the sacrifice of Christ on the cross at Calvary. Now his ultimate destruction is assured. We have been set free, if we so choose. Satan has truly fallen, and for him there is no redemption.

And yet he continues to try to lure people to disbelieve God and defy His purposes. Satan's plans remain the same. His intentions now are the same as they were at the time of his fall from God's grace:

> For you said in your heart, I will ascend into heaven, I will exalt my throne above the stars of God: I will sit also upon the mount of the congregation, in the sides of the north; I will ascend above the heights of the clouds; I will be like the Most High. (Isa.14:13–14)

In his pride, Satan has still not accepted the sovereignty of God over all things. He still does not accept his role as a created being—and one not created in the image of God. Satan is still perpetuating the lie of evolution as part of his strategy to deceive mankind into following him rather than Christ: Therefore rejoice, you heavens, and you that dwell in them. Woe to the inhabiters of the earth and of the sea! for the devil is come down to you, having great wrath, because he knows that he has but a short time (Rev.12:12).

If we continue to believe the lies of Satan and to devalue our status as image bearers of God, then we are, by default, image bearers of Satan. We follow his agenda and not God's. Belief in evolution changes our God-given status.

Some people will be drawn to the dangerous path that can lead to the attractive potential of transhumanism, which seeks eternity and perfection through human effort alone. If you can now recognize the danger, then please consider the door that Christ has opened for you. Satan's legacy can show you where not to go.

# CHAPTER 3

## Rebellion and Apostasy

Jesus says to him, I am the way, the truth and the life; no man comes to the Father, but by Me.

—John 14:6

Now we have seen the role of Satan in trying to subvert the human race in defiance of God, it is time to consider the outworking of the rebellion that has ensued and to see where it leads.

So, imagine walking through a forest, paths leading off in many directions. How would you know which way to go? What method would you choose to walk the right way towards your goal? Would you follow a map? Or look for the path that is way marked with a sign? Perhaps you would simply `follow your nose` and choose the most inviting and attractive looking path. Would you choose a narrow or a wide path? You have a lot of choice, but if it's the path of life that you are looking for, make sure it's the right one.

The path that began by leading out of the Garden of Eden is the path of human destiny. Eternal perfection has become mortal imperfection, but with the promise of restoration (Gen.3:14–15).Once-perfect creation is now marred by sin and under the curse of God:

> ...Cursed is the ground for your sake; in sorrow shall you eat of it all the days of your life; Thorns also and thistles shall it bring forth to you; and you shall eat the herb of the field; In the sweat of your face shall you eat bread, till you return to the ground; for out of it you were taken; for dust you are, and to dust shall you return. (Gen.3:17–19)

Countless times, God's name has been cursed because we live in a far from perfect world. Countless people have refused to trust in Him because of the suffering and hardship the world produces. Yet it is mankind that has brought about this situation. And even here, in the midst of judgement, God shows mercy:

> For the creature was made subject to vanity, not willingly, but by reason of Him who has subjected the same in hope. Because the creature itself also shall be delivered from the bondage of corruption into the glorious liberty of the children of God. For we know that the whole creation groans and travails in pain together until now. And not only they, but ourselves also, which have the first-fruits of the Spirit, even we

> ourselves groan inside ourselves, waiting for
> the adoption, that is, the redemption of our
> body. (Rom.8:20–23)

These verses show us several things. God created us. We 'come from dust and return to dust'. Not through the animal kingdom and not from any other way. God has spoken and informed us who we are. We turned away from God, and we are responsible for the ills of the earth. The blame lies at the feet of mankind. God has shown mercy and has revealed the path on which we can walk, if we choose to turn back to Him. Our rebellion lies in our refusal and denial. At some point in our lives, we've all been there.

There is one major difference between a believer and a nonbeliever. A believer has received forgiveness, while a nonbeliever hasn't. The believer is not a better person than the nonbeliever, but the believer is inwardly transformed. This is not a state that can be achieved through any means other than what Christ has done.

Advocates of theistic evolution try to have their cake and eat it too. But merging evolution and scripture does not negate the fact that the sovereignty of God, His authority, and even His character are being questioned. Subconsciously or not, the echo of the voice of Satan is heard in the recesses of the mind. A question like "Did God really say?" will likely lead to the conclusion that self knows best: I am the authority, I can only trust myself.

This denial of God in favour of self can be seen in the intentional steering of technology and society, towards transhumanism. This is an attempt to achieve perfection and immortality through the natural man rather than through the supernatural gift of God. It must be stated, however, that not all evolutionists follow the path that leads to transhumanism. Neither do all advocates of theistic evolution follow transhumanism. The route of transhumanism is really embedded in atheism. The danger for theistic evolutionists is that they will allow themselves to be deceived and attracted by atheism's claims.

Humanity has arrived at this point by blindly following the plans of Satan. Without God, we are pawns in Satan's strategies, listening to his words of deceit. His voice calls to us through the centuries, even from the Garden of Eden and his fateful conversation with Eve.

After that, mankind became degenerate. People became violent and uncaring, with hearts and minds full of wickedness—so much so that only the intervention of God stopped it in its tracks:

> And God saw that the wickedness of man was great in the earth, and that every imagination of the thoughts of his heart was only evil continually. And it repented the Lord that He had made man on the earth, and it grieved Him at His heart. And the Lord said, I will destroy man whom I have created from the face of the earth; both man, and beast, and the creeping thing, and the fowls of the air; for it repents Me that I have made them. But Noah found grace in the eyes of the Lord (Gen.6:5–8).

This is generally believed to have occurred only 1,656 years after creation week. Evil grew rapidly, in a way similar to the way that weeds grow quickly and choke all the good produce that grows from the soil.

Technology must have been advanced at that time. All God's specific instructions were followed precisely in building the ark that kept humanity safe throughout the terrific convulsions of the planet for the duration of the Flood. Only the gracious protection and providence of God brought them to a place of safety. That judgement is well documented throughout the world, not just in scripture, but in the historical records of different cultures. Evidence of this worldwide flood is widely available for all to see, when the millions of years spectacles that people wear, metaphorically speaking, are replaced with thousands of years spectacles. Again, metaphorically speaking. There are many books and websites on this subject, some of which I have named in the recommended reading list at the end of this book.

After the Flood, Noah and his family were confronted with an alien world far different from the one that had been destroyed. All animal and bird life was gone, apart from the creatures that came off the ark. Noah's family were the only people alive. It was a very inhospitable world, and they were alone in it. It's hard to imagine what that felt like.

What did Noah do? Did he scream, rant, and rage, shaking his fist at God? No, he built an altar to the Lord (Gen.8:20). He knew that God had saved them from an evil and degenerate world, and had shown love and mercy. Noah trusted his Creator.

Noah followed all of God's instructions and was totally obedient to Him. This could have been a new beginning.

This was the path that should have been followed. But Noah's family still had within them a sinful nature, which gradually overruled the voice of God and led them down the path that Satan had begun. They went their own way. What happened then?

Approximately one hundred years after the Flood, all of Noah's sons had large families and were grandfathers and great-grandfathers. Their family tree is recorded in Genesis 10. Noah's son Ham had a son whose name was Cush, who fathered a son called Nimrod: And Cush fathered Nimrod: he began to be a mighty one in the earth ... and the beginning of his kingdom was Babel, and Erech, and Ac`cad, and Cal`neh, in the land of Shinar' (Gen.10:8, 10).

The character of Nimrod can be recognized from his name, which means 'let us rebel'. His character revealed that he was heavily under the influence of Satan. Nimrod is considered by many theologians to be a type of Antichrist who, as prophetically recorded in God's Word, will reign over the entire earth during the end times.

It was at this time that apostasy and rebellion began to flourish. A civilization was established which consisted of most if not all of mankind. Nimrod was the recognized leader. He would have been head of a new world order, a one-world government. There was one language, so communication for all people would have been easy. However, they were all openly defying God, who had previously commanded them to 'be fruitful, and multiply and replenish the earth' (Gen.9:1), exactly as He had commanded Adam and Eve. Noah's descendants did not do this. Instead they began to build the Tower of Babel:

And the whole earth was of one language,
and of one speech. And it came to pass, as
they journeyed from the east, that they found
a plain in the land of Shi`nar; and they dwelt
there. And they said one to another, Go to, let
us make brick, and burn them thoroughly,
and they had brick for stone, and slime had
they for mortar. And they said, Go to, let us
build us a city and a tower, whose top may
reach to heaven; and let us make us a name,
lest we be scattered abroad upon the whole
face of the earth (Gen. 11:1–4).

In this new civilization, they chose to worship many
gods, and built images of nature, such as stars, the moon, the
sun, and animals. Nature worship replaced the worship of
the one who had created them. This pattern has continually
been repeated through the centuries.

The Tower of Babel was made as a monument to
reach the heavens. It was an astrological worship centre
to exalt creation rather than the Creator. All the people
were together, so evil quickly thrived. Their new civilization
became degenerate like civilization before the Flood (to a
lesser degree.) So again, God intervened by confusing their
language: And the Lord said "behold, the people is one, and
they have all one language; and this they begin to do: and
now nothing will be restrained from them, which they have
imagined to do. Go to, let Us go down, and there confound
their language, that they may not understand one another's
speech. (Gen.11:6-7). If God had not acted, mankind would
likely have destroyed itself, with no hope of redemption.

When reading the book of Genesis, you might notice the decline from monotheism – the worship of one God- to polytheism – the worship of many gods. It started with open rebellion against the one true God, to choosing who or what to worship in the natural world or the heavens. Nature gods were abundant within the spheres of paganism and pantheism. It gave Mankind a choice, or a preference. Many gods were worshipped simultaneously, depending on the mood and circumstances of the time. From the dispersion from the Tower of Babel to the worship of many idols in ancient Greece, it becomes clear that Mankind has sought to be 'divorced' from our Holy God. It is natural for humanity to worship. We were created to worship. However, all worship of anything or anyone, apart from our creator God, sends us down the wrong path.

Astrology became popular in the time of Nimrod and it is interesting to note the association of these "star gods" that they apparently worshipped, and the Nephilim. The Nephilim are considered to be the hybrid offspring between some fallen angels and human females. This is noted in many legends and cultures, particularly those of Greece. The Apocrypha book of Enoch is another. It becomes likely that it was fallen angels and their offspring that were also worshipped as gods. Many theologians are of the opinion that the intention of the fallen angels and of course, Satan, was to contaminate the seed (DNA) of humanity. This would have been the evil intent to negate the judgement of God upon Satan, as it would have prevented Jesus coming as Saviour. The pure line of humanity created in the image of God would have been destroyed. The events at the dispersion carried their rebellion forward.

Historians have placed these events at Babel approximately 110 years after the worldwide Flood. As evil rapidly permeated the human race between the Fall and the Flood, so it rapidly permeated the hearts and lives of the generations after the Flood. (Transhumanism is also a continuation of the attempt to corrupt mankind in the image of God, as we will see later.)

Until the confusion of languages and consequential spreading out of people groups (taking their apostate religions with them), human beings had apparently utilized the knowledge of technology they had previously had. (Note that they had the capability to build the high tower and astrological artifices.) This changed after the dispersion. People moved into unfamiliar territories and had to form new ways to govern themselves, as they were no longer under the leadership of Nimrod. Some of these new communities would have faced more challenges than others, depending on the terrain that they travelled. To start with, they may not have been able to use the technological skills they already had until such time as manpower and adequate resources became available. This may explain the popular view that humans were once primitive 'cavemen'. Once communities became established, they were again able to exercise their technological prowess. It is possible that their worship became incorporated into their culture and consequently the once God given ability to creatively utilize technology to sustain themselves and build new societies became a means of active rebellion against the true God of humanity.

Egypt had hundreds of deities that have been discovered by archaeologists and historians. Apostasy thrived and was still thriving during Jesus' human life, after His resurrection, and following the time of the early apostles. This was some two thousand years after the dispersion at the Tower of Babel. The Greek city of Athens is one well-known example of this: Now, while Paul waited for them at Athens, his spirit was stirred in him, when he saw the city wholly given to idolatry (Acts 17:16).

In one form or another, apostasy and idolatry continue to thrive today. Human philosophy replaces the truth of God's Word. The fact of sin is largely ignored. The world spirals rapidly into confusion and chaos alongside the escalation of violence, war, and acts of terrorism. Technology has not brought us peace alongside the benefits it has brought to our affluent lifestyles in the West. Neither has it brought an end to the hardships experienced in third world countries.

This situation is not the fault of technology. It is the fault of the sin that we all have. It is the fault of humanity, who is unable to use technology in a perfect manner.

The pursuit of transhumanism follows a path parallel to the path of early civilizations after the events of Babel. We can mimic the path they chose for themselves, or we can learn from their error. Do we elevate ourselves, or do we elevate God? Is God to be worshipped or is mankind to be worshipped? Do we exercise faith in God or faith in what technology can do for us? Do we put our faith in transhumanism?

In many ways, we can look at how God dealt with and continues to deal with the nation of Israel. That should be our example. To see how He responded to their apostasy and their rebellion. This is something that is extensively documented throughout scripture.

Apostasy has always been affected by the filtering of God's Word. We fail in our walk with Christ by watering down His life-giving Word to embrace our own less-than-perfect human words that are undeniably tainted by our fallen condition. Instead of regarding the holiness of His Word as our strong fortress and tower, we weaken our defences by embracing popular trends. This was the error of Israel in the past, and is our current situation today.

God dealt with Israel with warnings, followed by judgement in the times when warnings went unheeded. He will deal with us accordingly. Israel embraced the idolatry surrounding her, and we are doing the same. Apostasy today is open rebellion in matters of sexual orientation, abortion, and many other areas of modern society. It is leading to open warfare over our very humanity.

To be human is to be created in the image of God. Transhumanism is the merging of man and machine, and is likely to benefit from a genderless society. Transhumanism is, however, being confused with our general use of technology. Of course, this is something that Satan loves, as he is the author of chaos and confusion. Rather than using technology as a tool, as we have done in the past, transhumanism is leading us to dependency upon technology—a form of enslavement. Before long, we will not be able to live without it.

That puts those of the Christian faith in direct confrontation with our holy and perfect God. There are some Christians who suggest that transhumanism is 'helping' Jesus Christ. But why would the Creator ever need our help? Others suggest that transhumanism is the means that God has chosen to make us perfect. But the cross of

Jesus is already about redemption and reconciliation. It is to do with making the human spirit alive in Christ and sealing the eternal destiny of the human soul.

Only God's grace can bring this hope to fruition. It is His accomplishment alone. We are required to trust Him and have faith in Him. It is not something to be accomplished by any human works whatsoever, and is not something that we can add to. It is not God's way to evolve us to a higher and more perfect species, but to bring about our original perfection. God's way is to reconcile what was lost.

Before the Fall, humanity was perfect and our relationship with God was perfect. That relationship was lost and cannot be regained through transhumanism. We lost that perfect relationship because of sin. Sin is like a great, impenetrable wall that cannot be assailed by mankind. Dealing with sin is the root struggle of every individual, and it is through God's way alone that it can be dealt with, despite all human efforts to avoid it. Hope in transhumanism is merely apostasy in modern form. If we don't submit fully to the authority and sovereignty of Christ, we will lose our way.

# CHAPTER 4

## Losing the Way

He said to them, But whom say you that I
am? Peter answering said, The Christ of God.

—Luke 9:20

The saddest thing that the worldview of atheistic evolution
brings is the conscious or subconscious thought that when
we die, we cease to exist. In this view, human beings are
nothing more than a higher intelligent mammal. This life
is all there is.

The confusion that may result from merging this view
with Christianity can make Salvation appear less defined. It
becomes easier and perhaps seems more logical to embrace
transhumanism as an acceleration of the evolutionary
process, part of God's plan for mankind. The person of Jesus
Christ defined in God's Word becomes seriously distorted.

Such has happened within the Christian transhumanist
lobby. It was both interesting and sad to read the Christian
transhumanist viewpoint given by Micah Redding in his

article in the Huffington post entitled 'Christianity is Transhumanism' (https://huffingtonpost.com/micah-redding/ christianity-is-transhuma-b-9266542.html). Inside this article he talks of grace, and the fact that we all live by grace. No problem there. However, God's grace bestowed on believers is far greater and powerful than the grace we may extend to one another. It is different to the grace he believes is bestowed on us by generations of ancestors. God's grace does not come through works. It is not something we can earn. God's grace is given freely to those who believe that Jesus is the Son of God, and both fully God and fully Man. We are under God's grace only through believing in Jesus Christ as Lord and Saviour through His sacrifice for our sin. God's grace has nothing to do with human works, but everything to do with sin, and forgiveness. Scripture affirms this: For by grace are you saved through faith; and that not of yourselves: it is the gift of God: Not of works, lest any man should boast. (Ephesians 2:8-9). Grace is our standing before God: By whom also we have access by faith into this grace wherein we stand, and rejoice in hope of the glory of God (Romans 5:2).

The article appears not to incorporate the 'sin factor' and consequently appears to re-define who Jesus really is, and the purpose of His coming.

This is an interpretation of scripture from a worldly perspective that has not factored sin into the equation. It gives an out-of-focus picture of who Jesus Christ is and why He dwelt among those He created. It misses the point of His deity as the Son of God, and the reason for His crucifixion—atonement for our sin.

Jesus bore the crucifixion for our spiritual well-being and not for our material well-being. This might be interpreted in a way that means Christians are exempt from the suffering and hardships that non-Christians endure. But this is not the case. Jesus said, But rather seek you the kingdom of God; and all these things shall be added to you (Luke 12:31). Spiritual needs are addressed first, and then our physical needs.

The adversity human beings experience is primarily the consequence of sin. Jesus does care about our physical needs, but He cares for our spiritual needs much more.

The viewpoint that supports the physical condition above the spiritual condition appears to address scripture as human-centred through works rather than Christ-centred through His works. Let's take another look at Jesus:

> And now, O Father, glorify You Me with Your own self with the glory which I had with You before the world was. (John 17:5)

> And the Word was made flesh, and dwelt among us. (And we beheld His glory, the glory as of the only begotten of the Father,) full of grace and truth. (John 1:14)

Jesus is so much more than some Christian transhumanists envisage. What is a plausible explanation for this to happen? Perhaps when we give our world view the ultimate authority, we tend to try to merge scripture with that world view. We become vulnerable to the lies of Satan that undermine God's total authority and sovereignty. In one way or another, we are all susceptible to this. However, it is a dangerous path to follow. The end result is the same as when scripture is merged into the theory of evolution. It loses its inerrant value, and it is easier for us to get lost.

Later I will look at the technology that leads to transhumanism, and how our image of God becomes compromised. That happens when technology crosses the line to make us more than the human beings we were created to be. Remember, it is our fallen state that has caused our current limitations, and not the lack of technology. It makes sense to address the root cause of our current limitations, which is sin, rather than to merely mask the symptoms with our advanced use of technology.

The author Lawrence J Terlizzese makes some interesting remarks in his book *"Into the Void"* He points out that technology shapes the human conception of itself and its relationship to the world, including our view of God. It is an interesting point as it echo's a similar point made by Micah Redding in the aforementioned article in the Huffington post. Mr Redding's point was that our desire to advance science and technology is as much a spiritual exercise as it is a material one.

When we identify ourselves as created by God, our worldview is shaped by our relationship with Him in preference to our relationship with the world. Obviously our relationship with the world is still important. However, He should be foremost regarding our pre-occupation and concern. When that concept is not there, we look to something else. It appears that currently we are motivated towards funnelling a great deal of resource into the cause of advancing artificial intelligence through various means.

As Mr Terlizzese mentions, as our human relationships are reduced to efficiency, usefulness or convenient arrangements, we think of ourselves as machines.

I could not agree more. It seems that we are gradually coerced into thinking and conducting our affairs in a machine – like manner. Out inter-action with machines are currently voluntary but this is already changing and becoming more compulsory.

Mr Terlizzese recognizes that transhumanism takes that mechanistic view to the ultimate level of altering humanity – to become a machine. He also acknowledges that mankind is trying to control its evolutionary process to reach a perfectible state.[1]

This society appears to be heading towards dehumanising itself. Instead of communicating with people, we now have more opportunity to communicate via machine. Instead of holding a face-to-face conversation, we can text or send messages on Facebook or Twitter. We can voicelessly communicate without any reference to the person we are addressing. Human beings become digital 'friends' without having met. We don't see the body language of others or hear the inflections in their voices or see their facial expressions. Such interaction is impersonal. Communicating via a webcam with a person who is far away is a good thing, particularly if the communication is with a loved one, but I'm sure that most parents would prefer to see their sons and daughters in their presence rather than on a screen.

---

[1] L. J. Terlizzese *Into The Void: The Coming Transhuman Transformation* (Cambridge, Ohio: Probe Ministries: Christian Publishing House*, 2016), 45–6.

Our daily interactions with others are lessened through internet banking and shopping. This is useful in some respects, but lacks the person-centred approach. We are becoming accustomed to interacting with machines more than people. It is harder to express our personalities and tends to take the 'being' out of human beings.

Elderly people are becoming increasingly isolated. Many do not go out to shop because they are unaccustomed to current technologies. For their generation, before technology 'took over' a more personalized society was the normal way of life. One that involved more inter-action than life experienced today. Now, many stay at home and quite often, will see no-one.

In blindly accepting and following the dictates of our 'enlightened' society, do we consider the risk that this path is taking us further away from Christ? Are we losing the concept of love?

> As the Father has loved Me, so have I loved you: continue you in My love. If you keep my commandments, you shall abide in My love; even as I have kept My Father' commandments, and abide in His love (John 15:9–10).

> This is My commandment, That you love one another, as I have loved you (John 15:12).

These words clarify the way Jesus intends us to love Him and one another. Once we are conditioned to the secular world view of communication, which favours a more distant, impersonal kind of love, we are less likely to pursue a personal relationship with our Saviour.

Jesus' love is not intended as a conditional love, as it is sometimes interpreted through our earthly perception of the word *love*, expressed mainly through our emotions. The love that Jesus speaks of is both earthly and spiritual. It is a concern for our physical and spiritual welfare. This is consistent with His heavenly status as Son of God, combined with His earthly status as Son of Man.

When we are in Jesus' presence, as believers in Him and His teaching, we are able to bathe in that love and share it with others. When we are out of relationship with Him, we are hindered in experiencing that love and sharing it with others. Thus it is important to abide in His love. This love is expressed through relationship: from Father to Son to us, then from us to Christ to the Father, then outwardly from us to others.

Love in this respect leads the way to meaningful relationships and friendships, not the impersonal relationships that we seem to be experiencing more and more in our society. It is our increasing dependency that is taking us along this path, and not the use of technology as such. We seem to have moved away from the concept of using technology practically to help our efficiency. Dependency is quite different from simply using a tool. Even young children are being encouraged to use technology in 'play'. Some of them are likely to become participators in transhumanism in later life, because for them it would be a normal progression from something that they have grown up with.

Lack of love and impersonal relationships are not the signs of a stable nation, but on the contrary, an unstable nation. We are not living the utopian future that some transhumanists desire and tempt us with.

The kingdom of God is a lot different. It offers perfect love, perfect relationships, perfect health, and an eternal life with Him. It is through God's way and God's wisdom that this will be accomplished, not through human effort and human wisdom. Inevitably we risk losing an important aspect of the image of God, who, after all, is the Originator of love. It is another example of how we can lose our way on an increasingly rocky journey away from the safety of scripture.

There are many alternatives for those who choose not to walk with Christ. Let's take another look at what transhumanism offers.

Billionaire, futurist and entrepreneur, Elon Musk is well publicised as founding the Neuralink Corporation. The purpose of this facility (or one of its purposes), is the development of a neural lace that will interface directly with the brain. It is proposed to give the recipient thought control and the ability to merge with software. Mr Musk has often expressed concerns about the "Singularity". The "Singularity" is a term used, that has been given to the point in time when artificial intelligence, that is-general artificial intelligence (GAI), equals that of human intelligence through self learning processes. Human intelligence is then superseded by artificial intelligence that becomes super artificial intelligence (SAI). Interfacing through neural lace technology then becomes the means to keep pace with the escalating SAI.[2]

---

[2] A good book to read on this topic is James Barrat: *Our Final Invention: Artificial Intelligence and the end of the Human Era*, 1st edn. (St Martin's Griffin NY: 2013.)

Elon Musk has publicly spoken in the past months that his 'neural lace' would interface directly with the brain, letting the person communicate thoughts to computers (i.e., thought control) as an alternative to using a keyboard and mouse.[3]

The potential to control artificially intelligent robots with a mere thought is chilling. People with evil thoughts could wreak havoc on unsuspecting victims. No one could live in safety with his neighbour. We all tend to think bad thoughts about others at times, even when we don't really mean it. How would we rationalise that to a machine? We would all be at the mercy of another person's will. Think of how such a scenario would work in the hands of terrorists or so-called superpowers. This could well be a road to destruction that Satan loves. Such technology could be useful for those with physical limitations, but no one is perfect enough to prevent abuses.

Above all, the sin factor is ignored. If we believe we can have perfect thoughts and perfect human will, we are wrong. We are deceiving ourselves. It is God's will we must follow, and He does not wish us harm.

Other transhumanists have a different agenda. They are seeking immortality. Ray Kurzwell of Google fame is well known to be a strong proponent of this. Imagine a super-intelligent artificial life form that is self-repairing and freed from the restraints of biological decay. Imagine a utopia free from sickness and suffering. Imagine a man-made heaven with no conscience of what is right or wrong, no holy God to obey, and, of course, no judgement. Man would be his own god.

---

[3] From comments made at Recode's Code Conference, 2016.

The problem is that evil begets evil. With no restraint and, in effect, eternal earthly life, we are confronted with the very reason that Adam and Eve were commanded not to eat of the tree of good and evil:

> But of the tree of the knowledge of good and evil, you shall not eat of it: for in the day that you eat thereof you shall surely die. (Gen.2:17)

> And the Lord God said, Behold, the man is become like one of Us, to know good and evil: and now, lest he put forth his hand, and take also of the tree of life, and eat, and live for ever: Therefore the Lord God sent him forth from the garden of Eden, to till the ground from where he was taken. (Gen.3:22–23)

Why is it in our sinful nature to seek to be our own god? Perhaps, deep within us, we have this knowledge of the eternal. We know we are in rebellion against our Triune God and that we should acknowledge Him and worship Him. Instead we choose to worship self. We make ourselves a counterfeit god and seek our mortality in our own likeness because there is a need deep within us to worship something or someone. This reflects the way we are created in God's image—to worship Him. It is the first commandment:

> You shall have no other gods before me. You shall not make to you any graven image, or any likeness or any thing that is in heaven

above, or that is in the earth beneath, or
that is in the water under the earth: You
shall not bow down yourself to them, nor
serve them. (Exod.20:3–4)

You shall love the Lord your God with all
your heart, and with all your soul, and with
all your strength, and with all your mind;
and your neighbour as yourself. (Luke 10:27)

We have all fallen short of this at some point in our
lives, but we can see what a dangerous path it is to embrace
the ideals of transhumanistic philosophy, which appear so
contrary to scripture. It may not be a problem for those in
the embrace of atheism, but it should be a focus of concern
to those seeking the Christian faith. We are told not to make
any graven image—which surely comes under the umbrella of
a human-like artificial intelligence—nor to serve an image—
which is a possibility if transhumanists achieve their goals—
nor to bow down to them, which means to depend on them
rather than God. In all points, this is losing the way.

We seem to lose our identity when we cease to follow
Christ. After all, in distancing ourselves from Him, we are
not following His design for us. We are not only physical
beings but spiritual ones, and we have been designed to have
a close relationship with God. That is where our true identity
lies. If a relationship with Him doesn't drive us, something
else will. This other driver isn't necessarily technology; it
could be wealth, status, material possessions, looks, a job, or
anything else of this earth. But something will drive us, and
it will drive us away from God, as it has done in the past.

A counterfeit identity is not sufficient. But if we do not accept our true identity in Christ, then a counterfeit self will be all we have. It will never satisfy. The futile cry of 'who am I?' will not be fulfilled. Our true identity may be discarded, but it cannot be replaced. It can be regained solely through repentance and reconciliation through the sacrifice of Jesus Christ on the cross at Calvary.

In order to understand our own identity, it helps to look at God's identity. In doing this, we will understand more where transhumanism intends to lead us and why we should not go there. Let's take a look at the identity of God in the context of the Triune Godhead—three in one. He has some unfathomable characteristics that are totally unique.

> He is omniscient, with all-embracing knowledge:

> O the depths of the riches both of the wisdom and knowledge of God! How unreachable are His judgements, and His ways past finding out! (Rom.11:33)

> Such knowledge is too wonderful; it is high, I cannot attain to it. (Ps.139:6)

> He is omnipresent, present everywhere simultaneously:

> Where shall I go from your Spirit? Or where shall I flee from Your presence? If I ascend up into heaven, you are there; if I

make my bed in hell, behold, You are there.
(Ps.139:7–8)

He is omnipotent, all-powerful:

In the beginning God created the heaven
and the earth. (Gen.1:1)

To whom then will you liken Me, or shall
I Be equal? (Isa.40:25)

Have you not known? Have you not heard,
that the everlasting God, the Lord, the
Creator of the ends of the earth, faints not,
nor is weary? There is no searching of His
understanding. (Isa.40:28)

He is eternal, from everlasting to everlasting. He has
always existed and always will.

(Eternity for mankind in the realm of space, time, and
flesh is impossible, (1Cor.15:50). However, when time and
space are ended as we know them, at the return of Christ,
we will be given eternal bodies fit for heaven or hell. Those
who have chosen not to follow Christ will have a body fit
for Hell, whilst those who have chosen to follow Christ, will
be given a body fit for Heaven.)

These qualities of the Godhead are immutable. They are
not available for Mankind to take for himself. Nonetheless,
these are the characteristics that appear to be the goals that
transhumanists are seeking for themselves.

Through the merging of the human mind with an
artificial intelligent network, omniscience and omnipresence

are being pursued. This would give the merged mind power over every person who is connected. In theory at least, this merged mind could set itself up as a type of antichrist, if not *the* Antichrist.

How important it is to eat and drink of the living Word of God!

Our identities lie in the grace and provision of God, who graciously gives us His own characteristics when we are indwelt by the Holy Spirit at the point of Salvation, at the moment we are reconciled to God. These are the fruits of the Spirit, which become a work in progress by the indwelling Holy Spirit as we grow and mature into the conformity of Christ. These godly characteristics are the fruits of the Spirit: 'But the fruit of the Spirit is love, joy, peace, longsuffering, gentleness, goodness, faith, meekness, temperance: against such there is no law' (Gal.5:22–23).

This is in direct contrast to our earthly identity that consists of DNA, emotions, circumstances, and preferences. This kind of identity is the driving force of transhumanism rather than the identity that we have been designed by God to have.

Although apostasy, scriptural confusion, the lies and deceit of Satan, and our own sinful nature have led us to take less-than-perfect paths, Jesus still reigns and His Word remains steadfast and unchanging, like an anchor in the storm. We can weather the storms that loom on the horizon if we willingly make Jesus Christ the centre and focus of our lives.

Transhumanism sets itself against God. It is not too late to turn around and go back to Him. We may have lost the way, but Jesus is the Shepherd who looks for His lost sheep. If we call, He will come and gently draw us back to Him. We may be lost, but we don't have to stay lost.

# CHAPTER 5

*Copying God*

For you formed my inward parts; you covered me in my mother's womb. I will praise you for I am fearfully and wonderfully made; marvellous are your works, and that my soul knows well.

—Psalm 139:13–14

When God (Elohim) is acknowledged as Creator, the way we look at the world around us is transformed. We recognise the infinite power, wisdom, and knowledge of our Almighty God. It beckons us to know Him better. It tantalises us to understand how He thinks and how He does things. The concept of science is born, to 'think God's thoughts after Him' A well known quote. (Johannes Kepler, 1571–1630)

Carl Linnaeus (1707 – 1778), was a Swedish scientist well known for his love and belief in a Creator God. He is fondly remembered as the Father of Taxonomy – the Science of plant and animal classification. He saw the orderliness and design of God's Creation. One of his famous quotations is the *Nemesis Divina*, (1734):

Theologically, man is to be understood as the final purpose of the creation; placed on the globe as the masterpiece of the works of Omnipotence, contemplating the world by virtue of sapient reason, forming conclusions by means of his senses, it is in His works that man recognizes the Almighty Creator, the all-knowing, immeasurable and eternal God, learning to live morally under His rule, convinced of the complete justice of His Nemesis.[1]

> (The term 'Nemesis' has the meaning of
> the' inescapable judgement for sin'.)

It is because we are created in His image that we have the ability to understand the means that He used to create the physical realm in which we live. It is the use of His wisdom that is in view for us to see and learn by.

> (A good Bible text to read on the subject of
> God's wisdom is Proverbs 8:22-31.)

Science was summed up by Sir Francis Bacon, who is credited with the formation of the scientific methods of induction, deduction, hypothesis, and empirical proof that are followed today in general science. He was also a devout Christian.

The roots of science were a lot different to the way science is practised today. The world view of scientists, generally

---

[1] Linnacus c, *Nemesis Divinia; 1834* (as trans. By Michael John Petry 2001): Springer,21. https://en.wikiquote.org/wiki/Carl-Linnaeus

speaking, has shifted from God-centred to God-less centred. The awe and wonder of what God has accomplished has largely been replaced by what man has accomplished, with God out of the picture.

Although there is a dividing line between the world views based on creation and the theory of evolution, the desire to discover how everything works drives both perspectives. In the evolutionary world view, science and technology are the pursuit and utilisation of knowledge, fuelled by the premise that the world has existed for millions of years. A young earth world view is based on the premise of creation having occurred in six days of twenty-four hours each.

The interpretation of data is influenced by which world view the interpreter follows. This in turn influences the manner in which scientific investigations progress. For instance, while studying the many systems that make up the human body, an evolutionist would perhaps refer to what he or she considers as previous life forms that have progressed to current life forms, envisaging all forms as part of an ongoing process towards future life forms, which of course, is a motivation for transhumanism.

A creationist however, would probably see the human body as the finished handiwork of God, as something that is complete and does not require improvement. He/she might see the necessity to use science and advanced technology as a means to repair the human body, but not to alter it to something it has not been created to be. This person would likely be of the opinion that the cause of human frailty was the consequences of the Fall, rather than a Holy God creating an imperfect human being. This view is consistent with the second law of thermodynamics i.e., a loss of order.

This is a completely different response to the worldview of an evolutionist.

One area of advancing technology is genetic engineering. It is pivotal to both the repair of the human body, and to the transhumanist agenda. Genetic research appears to be crossing the line by experimenting with hybrid human/animals. (Since the introduction of the Human Fertilisation Embryology Act, the mixing of animal and human genetic material is now legal.)

This is copying Satan and is part of his strategy, one that has similarities to attempt to de-humanise humans, such as the union of fallen angels and human females that produced the Nephilim. This event brought God's judgement upon the world by means of the well documented worldwide Flood. Mankind is still being deceived by Satan.

There does appear to be a gradual breakdown of genetic material within the human body. What is causing it?

'A build-up of genetic mutations over many generations results in today's humans being less fit. Each person has about a hundred more mutations than their parents. This genetic entropy means that our bodies and brains have deteriorated' (Dr David Rosevear, Creation Science Movement, Portsmouth: pamphlet 403 August 2016.)

One of the leaders of the relatively new field of computational neuroscience is Dr Richard Granger. He has created algorithms that mimic human brain circuits. Dr Granger appears to work on the premise that the human brain as something not evolved to perfection, having been tested by chance rather than design. Presumably, (my conjecture), the human brain is expected to become obsolete as the 'evolutionary brain' is superseded/replaced, by artificial intelligence. This view obviously does not recognise the wisdom of God in the creation of man, and should be something of consideration to Christians attracted by transhumanism.[2]

There is a warning in basing knowledge on man's wisdom rather than God's wisdom. If we cross the line to reinvent the human brain, we are seeking our own glory rather than acknowledging God's glory. We are, in effect, saying we can do better than Him, 'fulfilling the desires of the flesh and of the mind', leading to God's wrath against us (Eph. 2:3).

There are limits to what we should do. The boundary is crossed when the increase of knowledge becomes an idol in itself and elevated above the throne of God, until the pursuit of knowledge becomes the throne of man. To remember the following scripture verse is helpful to keep ourselves in our rightful place, and for Jesus to be kept in His rightful place: For the invisible things of Him from the creation of the world are clearly seen, being understood by the things that are made, even His eternal power and Godhead; so that they are without excuse (Rom. 1:20).

We have been given the ability to appreciate and admire God's handiwork in His originally unflawed design, and given the ability to copy it, but He has not given us the mandate to take our explorations and curiosity beyond His

---

[2] Information taken from J. Barrett, *Our Final Invention: Artificial Intelligence and the End of the Human Era,* 214-215 (1st St Martin's Griffin Edition. New York: Feb. 2015). The "Granger" being referenced is Dr Richard Granger, director of the Dartmouth University Brain Engineering Laboratory. He has created algorithms that mimic circuits in the human brain.

handiwork. After all, we are not gods. We can admire shape, colour, texture, and smell. We can appreciate the intricate workings of sight for the eye and sound for the ear, and to recognise beauty, diversity, and uniqueness, both in the human body and in the world of nature around us. We do have the mandate to acknowledge Him and give Him the glory for His handiwork.

How can we see and acknowledge the random, unplanned, chance results of evolution? When we admire a painting, architecture, or other intricate subject of man-made design, we give credit to its designer. How much more should we credit the original Designer?

We should remember our limitations. However, when the theory of evolution is followed, there are no limitations. This gives those who pursue transhumanism free rein to 'play god'. Additionally, we have little knowledge of the spiritual world that God has also created. We are spiritual as well as physical beings. We cannot emulate spirituality. We can only copy the physical world in which we live.

Human beings are more than a brain equipped with knowledge. We also need wisdom. God's wisdom is far greater than man's wisdom. In His wisdom, He has seen fit to keep the spiritual realm off limits to mankind. That's a good thing, because otherwise we would likely attempt to tamper with it, as we do with the body and the mind. We need to remember who God is and who we are.

A lot of the physiology and anatomy of the human body can be copied by scientific and technological endeavour. There are many books and articles to read on the subject. We now know the intricate processes of bone formation and growth, and the amazing ways in which the human skeleton is formed. We recognise irreducible complexity, in which every part is inter-dependent and working together, or else it doesn't work at all. This is evidence of intelligent design, which is the intelligence and wisdom of God. We must thank Him for making this information available to us and for giving us the ability to utilise it for good in our fallen state.

We should acknowledge workers in science and technology for their valuable contributions to humanity. This work, of course, takes a lot of perseverance and, probably, self-sacrifice. These workers have not achieved their goals by mere chance, although many believe that this is how the world came into existence. Their efforts did not evolve, but originated with a plan and a purpose.

However, it must be noted that God's master design of creation did not require team effort! All was accomplished merely by the Word of His mouth, with no assistance needed! In just five days of twenty-four hours each, He put all of our diverse ecosystems in place, to be governed by our recognised laws of nature. On the sixth day, He formed the intricate systems of the human body. After thousands of years, we still don't fully know how He did that. We are still learning!

God's work should inspire us, but we should not seek to replace it or attempt to make it more than God intended it to be. Sadly, that is what we are doing. Not content with utilising technology to repair the human body, we are now finding ways to give our bodies super abilities and super strength. This is something we shall look at shortly.

First, let's take a look at man's progress in copying God from nature (biomimetics). Copying God's intricate designs in nature gives us many benefits in our daily lives.

For instance, studying how birds and insects fly has assisted in the development of planes and helicopters. Chameleons have amazing eyes which have assisted in the development of lenses. If you wear a hearing aid or know someone who does, then thank the flies. They have inspired technologists to produce the fine tuning that some people need in order to have a clearer interpretation of sound*. The design of nautilus has given us submarine flotation tanks. Copying the design of the beak of the woodpecker has helped us design shock absorbers. Studying the echolocation abilities of bats and dolphins has given us sonar. These are just a few examples.

(Many detailed examples can be found in the book *By Design: Evidence for nature's Intelligent Designer- the God of the Bible:* Dr Jonathan Sarfati: creation book publishers,2008: also available from creation.com.)

Rather than glorify technology, we should glorify God:

The hearing ear, and the seeing eye, the Lord has made even both of them' (Prov.20:12).

> But ask now the beasts, and they shall teach you; and the fowls of the air, and they shall tell you; Or speak to the earth, and it shall teach you: and the fishes of the sea shall declare to you. Who knows not in all these that the hand of the Lord has wrought this? (Job 12:7–8)

The world view behind our use of technology should be carefully considered by Christians, when evaluating the attractiveness of transhumanism.

It was God who created communication, and it was God who first gave us the language to communicate with. Although humans originally spoke one language, it changed when God confused the one language into many. Now we can communicate without the need to learn a different language, through the means of translation. This technology has played its part in shrinking the planet but cannot touch on the communication between God and mankind.

Communication is a precious gift to us in order that we can have a one-to-one relationship with our Saviour. That aspect of communication cannot be copied. We cannot have a personal relationship with Him through any technological means. That is a line that cannot be crossed. We can copy the physical realm that God has given us, but the spiritual realm is out of bounds. The spiritual realm defies transhumanism. We cannot copy God Himself, and we cannot make ourselves gods. One day we will be fully in His image, but that will not require any form of transhumanism at all.

Sadly, we utilise God's design to create things that are destructive. Artificial intelligence (AI) is now taking steps to augment or even to replace the human brain. AI's proponents claim that AI can think for itself, through machine learning.

Those involved in producing transhumanist technologies appears to be on the road to self-destruction in order to avoid any godly intervention in their plans.

An article published by the BBC in 2017, voiced the concerns of robotic experts who were calling for a ban on the development of "killer robots". (It is already public knowledge that drones are used for surveillance), but further development enables a drone to destroy a target, (perhaps a living target). It appears there is concern regarding weapons controlled by AI rather than a person. The article points out that "smart tech" being unleashed by the arms industries will likely lead to a "third revolution in warfare". The article also mentions Kalashnikov's "neural net" combat module whose makers claim can make its own targeting judgement without human control. It can make its own decisions based on self learning ability.[3]

Exoskeletons are already proving useful for people with mobility issues. They can enable someone to walk again. They are also useful to assist in moving or carrying heavy loads in industry. However, imagine someone or a group of people who have taken this to the higher level of super strength-or enhanced strength. If this technology was used for a non-peaceful purpose, then would you be able to defend yourself or others in the event of a threat? If a neural implant was lodged in the brain giving enhanced and quicker thought processes, would you then be able to react fast enough? Or if enhanced vision and hearing was used, far and above the normal human capacity for sight and vision, would you be able to escape? It's not surprising that the "military machines" around the world are watching closely...

We can see how we have travelled down the road from imitating God's design to replacing His workmanship with our own. The implication is that we believe our workmanship is superior to His. In our arrogance, we ignore the fact that the original design was His, and still is. He has graciously allowed us copyright permission. This takes us further down the road to a confrontation with the Author and perfect Designer of everything that exists. There will be a day of accountability.

---

[3] M. Smith, Technology of Business reporter: Business: 'Is "killer robot" warfare closer than we think?', BBC News, 25 August 2017.

# CHAPTER 6

## Who Are You?

It is sown a natural body; it is raised a spiritual body...And so it is written. The first man Adam, was made a living soul, the last Adam was made a quickening spirit.

—1 Corinthians 15:44.45

If you were to travel on the wide road to destruction, whom would you meet? Probably those who look no different to yourself: friendly, caring people, a good friend or neighbour, some people who are hard-working and perhaps successful in life. Perhaps they would mostly be comfortable with themselves and pleased with their own achievements. Perhaps they would be happily cocooned within their society, protected by materialism and following a secular way of life, in which they share the illusion of safety and harmony.

Others would be following, trying to keep up, trusting that those in front know where they are going and that everybody is on the right road. This is the 'safety in numbers' belief that, in general, the media encourages us all to follow. 'If it's popular, it's OK.' Maybe that's true sometimes, but not always.

Jesus warns us to keep off this road. It's the wrong road. We should look to the narrow road:

> Enter you in at the strait gate: for wide is the gate, and broad is the way, that leads to destruction and many there be which go in there at: Because strait is the gate, and narrow is the way, which leads to life, and few there be that find it. (Matt.7:13–14)

The broad way is the wrong road because it is based merely on human effort, human value, and human control. We devalue ourselves on this road. We fail to see who we really are. We are so much more than who we think we are. We tend to forget that each of us has a soul and a spirit within, given by God. We tend to look only at what we can see with our eyes or perceive with our minds.

However, we are loved by Almighty God. We are created in His image. We are each of us unique, and of such value in the eyes of God that He gave His Son to die for us on the cross, that we might be forgiven. That's if we want to be forgiven. If we know we need to be forgiven. If we know that we are sinners.

That is why there is such busy activity on this road. We're looking everywhere but to the cross. We are denying Christ and what He has done. We are trying to save ourselves, justify ourselves, and pretend to ourselves that we can live without Christ. We can't, so we need to get off that road.

Transhumanism walks that road, under a banner that reads, 'Mankind can do it. We can be gods. We can live forever.' We need to see who we really are and to see our true potential in what God has given us in order to 'be'.

The human body is a masterpiece, which was once unflawed and perfect in every way. We can still see some of that perfection within ourselves, though now, some six thousand years on, it has deteriorated greatly from what it once was. Here is one example:

> A typical healthy human brain houses some 200 billion nerve cells, which are connected to one another via hundreds of trillions of synapses. Each synapse functions like a micro processor, and tens of thousands of them can connect a single neuron to other nerve cells. In the cerebral cortex alone, there are roughly 125 trillion synapses. This is about how many stars fill 1'500 Milky Way galaxies.[1]

This is just a tiny description of one important component of the wonderfully made human body, fashioned by God during the very first sixth day, during the very first week of existence for the material universe. Can the original

---

[1] *Creation Journal of the Creation Science Movement*: Portsmouth, UK: vol.19:2 May 2016. (journal available as back copy at www.csm.org.uk)

design really be improved upon? Is God to be mocked, that humanity thinks it can do better?

Dorcas Cheng-Tozun wrote a thought provoking article in Christianity Today magazine. The article was entitled 'The Imago Dei Meets Superhuman Potential'. The writer brings our attention to what it would mean when infallibility and mortality is no longer certain, and how such abilities would influence the ways in which we see ourselves, our relationships with one another, the rest of creation and most importantly – with God.

Attention is drawn to the question of who would have access to these life and mind enhancing technologies – and who wouldn't. Questions are raised regarding the physical and psychological traits of so called "designer humans".[2]

The problem to address here is that with regard to our inherent sinful nature. Most of us would like to think of ourselves as good people, or perhaps mostly - good people. We look at the morals, ethics and attitudes that we uphold and deem ourselves as "doing mostly ok". However, in actuality, we have defined the interpretation of the word "good" ourselves, and this to suit our own sense of satisfaction. We then put ourselves in the place of self justification.

The Collins English Dictionary (Harper Collins Publishers: Glasgow, uk: edn2008), says this on the word "justify/justification", 'to prove (a decision, action or idea), to be reasonable or necessary'. Compare this to the biblical use of the word. Biblically, it is God who justifies – who imparts righteousness to us when we are reconciled to Him through the Atoning work of Christ in paying the price for

---

[2] www.christianitytoday.com/ct/2016/march-web-only/imago-dei-meets-superhuman-potential-html

our sin. Imputed righteousness is when God declares us to be righteous. This word connects to the word "justification". It is found in both the Old and New Testaments. In the Old Testament the Hebrew word "sadaq" is used for "justification/justify" and refers to the term "made righteous". In the Greek translation of the New Testament, "dikaiosis" refers to the term "justification/justify" and also means "made righteous". It appears that only God can truly justify, and not we ourselves.

Therefore we can conclude that human nature referring to itself as good, is flawed. We make our own rules. Our inherent sinful nature-inherited from Satan- leads us to deceive ourselves. We decide what is good and what isn't. We decide what is justifiable and what isn't. So our own thinking is the bedrock for our motivation. Who decides how far transhumanism can go? Who would be the best person to follow? Perhaps within this framework we need to consider what God defines as "good". Sadly, we all fall short of His standard. We are not holy. We are not good. The sinful nature that every person has – with no exception – makes us susceptible to self centeredness, pride and greed, whether we like to admit it or not:

For all that is in the world, the lust (*strong desire*) of the flesh and the lust (*strong desire*) of the eyes, and the pride of life, is not of the Father, but is of the world. (1 John2:16.)

And He said, That which comes out of the man, that defiles the man. For from inside, out of the heart of men, proceed evil thoughts, adulteries, fornications, murders, Thefts, covetousness, wickedness, deceit, lasciviousness (*sensuality*), an evil eye, blasphemy (*slander*), pride, foolishness: All these evil things come from inside, and defile the man (Mark 8:20-23).

Would it be reasonable to expect an advanced 'superhuman' to have pure thoughts and motivations? To not be motivated by a sense of power and ultimate authority over others? To not be motivated by greed or selfish interests detrimental to others? How would weakness or imperfection be perceived? As we not gods we are not infallible. Self learning artificial intelligence would also learn these traits. They too, would not be perfect, or infallible. Rather than pursuing a utopian heaven, we could be pursuing a man made hell.

What about consciousness?

In his book "*The Case for a Creator*" journalist and author Lee Strobel investigates the fascinating concepts of consciousness. He points out the controversial question in Ray Kurzweil's book "*The Age of Spiritual Machines*"* of whether artificial intelligence can achieve consciousness. Mr Kurzweil appears to think so. Lee Strobel sees this theory as the logical extension of Darwinian evolutionary thought. Darwinists believe that the physical is all that there is, and the human brain evolved until it was able to develop subjectivity, feelings, hopes, rationality, reason and self awareness. This evolutionary thinking appears to surmise that if the automatic by-product of increasingly sophisticated brain power is the cause of consciousness, then what is stopping artificial intelligence from becoming conscious when their power exceed that of humans. An interesting but chilling thought.[3]

---

[3]  L. Strobel, *The Case for a Creator*: *A journalist investigates Scientific Evidence That Points Toward God.* (Grand Rapids, Michigan: Zondervan, 2004) 247-248.

* Ray Kurzweil, inventor, futurist, author: *Age of Spiritual Machines*, published 2001 by Viking, also Penguin NY, USA,1999.

So what is the brain? To some people, it is nothing more than a physical lump of meat, and consciousness merely a mechanical product governed by electrical impulses. To others, the brain is an evolved product that requires improvement. Still others believe the brain is a highly sophisticated organ and clearly the work of an intelligent Designer. Or is the brain part of a person created in the image of God, which has a spiritual dimension behind its function?.[4]

If evolution were true, how would consciousness and self-awareness arise from a lump of meat? Or to put it in a different way, how would life arise from nonlife? What connection is consciousness likely to have with the second law of thermodynamics—that is, the law of entropy? This question should be easily answered by those professing the Christian faith. The law of entropy is the consequence of sin. So the enigma of the human brain and consciousness can be found in the pages of scripture.

Before we explore this, I would like to share something with you from my own experience. I was privileged to be involved in the care of a 100-year-old lady at a nursing home. She had advanced dementia and did not know her own name, nor could she recognise herself. She needed assistance with all her personal needs. Yet this lady was one of the most Spirit-filled Christians I have ever met. She would continuously praise God, giving thanks to Him, her face aglow with happiness and love. She would look out the window and draw our attention to the fact that God made everything. She reminded us how much we should be grateful to Jesus, who gave His life for us. She kept us

[4] L. Strobel, *The Case for a Creator*, 250–1.

humble. We were also encouraged, as she showed us that God bypasses the brain to speak directly to the soul and spirit. A damaged brain is no obstacle to Him.

Our Triune God is Three in One. The Father is a Person, the Son is a Person, and the Holy Spirit is a Person. 1x1x1=1.

As an analogy, think of water. It can be liquid, it can be frozen, and it can be steam, but in every case it is still water. We too are three in one. We are body, soul, and spirit.

> I pray God your whole spirit and soul and body be preserved blameless to the coming of our Lord Jesus Christ. (1Thess.5:23)

> For the Word of God is quick and powerful, and sharper than any two edged sword, piercing even to the dividing asunder of soul and spirit, and of the joints and marrow and is a discerner of the thoughts and intentions of the heart (Heb.4:12).

We could describe the human body as the means by which we relate to the world around us. We use our senses— sight, smell and hearing, touch, and taste— as well as motor function, cognition, and imagination. Our brains help us to utilise our God-given abilities. The human body is full of complexity that is still not fully understood.

The soul is the seat of personality. It gives us self-awareness. It is immortal, whereas the physical body is not. As we know full well, the physical body decays and dies. Our spirits can be either dead or alive. The spirit too is immortal.

When we die, we receive the outcome of the decision we have made regarding Christ. When we are born, our immortal spirit is dead. That is because we are born separated from God. If that state is unchanged when the body dies, then the immortal soul, closely linked to the immortal spirit, will go to hell as its final destination.

On the other hand, the spirit can be made alive through reconciliation with God. If the person repents and receives forgiveness for sin, i.e., salvation through Christ, the immortal spirit and the immortal soul go to heaven as their final destination.

In either case, the personality remains the same, but with a new body fit for its place of residence. Contrary to the proclamations of evolution, we do not simply cease to exist when we die.

> Wherefore let them that suffer according to the will of God commit the keeping of their souls to Him in well doing, as to a faithful Creator (1 Pet.4:19).

> For whosoever will save his life shall lose it: and whosoever will lose his life for my sake shall find it. For what is a man profited, if he shall gain the whole world, and lose his own soul? For the Son of man shall come in the glory of His Father with His angels and then He shall reward every man according to his works (Matt.16:25–27).

> The Apostle Paul had something interesting to tell us which many theologians and

historians estimate that he wrote sometime between AD 55-57. He says:

While we look not at the things which are seen, but at the things which are not seen: for the things which are seen are temporal; but the things that are not seen are eternal (2 Cor 4:18).

This is interesting because it reminds us of the material world that we can see, in comparison to the immaterial world that we cannot see. We could surmise that it is the immaterial part of us that has precedence over our material body because it is the part of us that is immortal. Note that God is Spirit and in His image we must have a spiritual identity that images His own. Remember also, that He is immortal. Note also the following:

For we must all appear before the judgement seat of Christ; that every one may receive the things done in his body, according to that he has done, whether it be good or bad (2 Cor 4:10). It is not the human body that is judged, but our immortal soul.

Jesus confirms this in Luke 11:40. For even more confirmation, look at the events after the Crucifixion. It is recorded in all of the four Gospels of Mathew, Mark, Luke and

John. When the human body was lowered from the cross, He was pronounced dead, but obviously His spirit was conscious because He preached to the fallen angels that had sired the Nephilim. After we learn that Jesus was put to death in the flesh and made alive by the Spirit, we told this: By which also He went and preached to the spirits in prison; which sometime were disobedient, when once the long-suffering of God waited in the days of Noah, while the ark was a preparing, wherein few, that is, eight souls were saved by water (1Peter 4:18-20). We can see that the human spirit is conscious even when the body is dead. Therefore we can conclude that the seat of consciousness is not in the brain, but that the brain is more likened to 'software' being utilised by 'hardware'. As before Salvation, the human soul is sinful and thus imperfect, perfection cannot be achieved through self learning artificial intelligence. We can also conclude that consciousness begins at conception and that this confirms the beginning of the life of a person. Therefore we can consider ourselves in extreme error before God with the practice of terminating pregnancies.

Our sinful nature will not allow the technology to stop at medical benefits. It can also be turned to military use, as mentioned before. This advantage will enable wars to be fought and won. Many countries are possibly vying for this kind of technology in order to exercise power over others, both in defence and attack. The innate desire of degenerate man, apart from God, is to exercise authority over the world, to conquer, and to be our own gods. Degenerate humanity desires to follow the purposes of Satan, who is our ruler if we have not chosen Christ.

Why would any Christian be tempted by this future? Perhaps because they have allowed worldly influences to tempt them into following the advances of technology into transhumanism. Scripture warns us of this: But every man is tempted, when he is drawn away of his own lust, and enticed. Then when lust has conceived, it brings forth sin (Jas. 1:14–15). We are all tempted in every way, and once that happens, we are easily deceived by Satan to believe his lies.

Thankfully, we can resist and put on the armour that God has given us:

> Put on the whole armour of God, that you may be able to stand against the wiles of the devil, for we wrestle not against flesh and blood, but against principalities, against powers, against the rulers of the darkness of this world, against spiritual wickedness in high places. Wherefore take to you the whole armour of God, that you may be able to withstand in the evil day, and having done all, to stand. Stand therefore, having your loins girt about with truth, and having on the breastplate of righteousness: And your feet shod with the preparation of the gospel

> of peace; Above all, taking the shield of faith,
> wherewith you shall be able to quench all the
> fiery darts of the wicked. And take the helmet
> of salvation, and the sword of the Spirit,
> which is the word of God. (Eph.6:11–17)

So the danger that appears to be paramount for those of the Christian faith is threefold: not taking up the shield of faith: not putting on the helmet of salvation: and not taking up the sword of the Spirit, which is the living Word of God. The lies of Satan thereby deceive the Christian. The lie is that man's efforts can achieve God's desires, usurping His plans for those of secular mankind.

Thankfully, through repentance, we can ask for deliverance and restoration. Remember again who we are:

> It is sown a natural body; it is raised a
> spiritual body.There is a natural body and
> there is a spiritual body. And so it is written.
> The first man Adam, was made a living
> soul; the last Adam was made a quickening
> spirit. However that was not first which
> is spiritual, but that which is natural; and
> afterward that which is spiritual. The first
> man is of the earth, earthy; the second man
> is the Lord from heaven. As is the earthy,
> such are they also that are earthy: and as
> is the heavenly, such are they also that are
> heavenly. And as we have borne the image
> of the earthy, we shall also bear the image
> of the heavenly. (1 Cor.15:44–49)

Why substitute Jesus Christ for the kind of artificial, impersonal, technological future that transhumanism proposes? Our real future, according to God's plans and purposes, is much better!

To recap: Adam was made a living soul. The soul is separate from the brain. All the knowledge contained in the brain cannot save us from ourselves. It cannot provide us with everlasting happiness. It cannot provide us with everlasting peace. That is because the essence of humanity is in the soul and not in the brain.

It is through the soul that love exists—that is expressed in correlation to the brain. Uploading or downloading a human brain would increase knowledge but not love. It would not be the means to achieve perfect happiness or to execute perfect peace in perfect judgement.

Unlimited knowledge is unlikely to provide unsullied contentment or fulfilment, or the ability to perfectly love another person. It would be yet another false god to elevate self above the throne of God. That's Satan's purpose, so why follow him? Neither Satan nor his purposes can attain the perfection and holiness of God. Satan can never achieve the wisdom, mercy, grace, power and authority of God. Satan can never surpass God's abilities.

God alone is omnipresent and omniscient. He alone could bring everything into existence by the Word of His mouth. He alone could make man a living, conscious soul and breathe into him His own breath of spiritual life. No man or machine can do better.

The difference between what is obtainable through Christ and what is anticipated to be obtainable through transhumanism is that what Christ offers is through His

Grace, and what transhumanism offers is through human endeavour.

The problem, of course, is the overwhelming matter of sin. That is the most urgent consideration to settle for every individual. It is at the heart of the choice that everyone must make.

Will transhumanism achieve some of its goals? Many people believe it is likely. What man sets his heart to do, he will eventually do. This is a lesson that we can learn from the words of the Lord in Genesis 11:6.

Although the cause of medical research appears to be the driving force to implement the goals of transhumanism, the opposite is true as well. It appears to be possible to improve the health of the human body by less invasive means.

The following information is taken from an article on hyperbaric research by Xavier Figueroa:

> Hyperbaric oxygen therapy (HBOT) has been in use for over 100 years, safely treating a variety of medical conditions under increased pressure. By augmenting total gas pressure, oxygen levels in all body organs can be increased dramatically, sparing and maintaining organs that are oxygen deprived, removing obstructions in blood flow caused by gas bubbles, and inhibiting certain types of bacteria. The ability of HBOT to help in the healing process is mediated by a number of different mechanisms in the body. Each of these mechanisms helps us to understand why

> HBOT can accelerate wound healing and
> help in combating a variety of neurological
> diseases … HBOT has shown a beneficial
> effect in reducing inflammation in stroke
> and head trauma. This anti-inflammatory
> effect helps to reduce swelling and increase
> healthy blood flow to the brain. At the
> same time, HBOT promotes the growth
> of new blood vessels, increases the number
> of circulating stem cells that are involved
> in new blood vessel growth and wound
> healing and induces the production of new
> neurons in the brain.[5]

Given the encouragement towards better health and the non invasive approach that hyperbaric therapy offers, it is rather surprising that it does not get the equivalent media attention and government financial support currently enjoyed by technologies supporting the goals of transhumanism.

Perhaps one reason for this is that HBOT is more aligned to the biblical account of creation and the judgement of the worldwide Flood than the evolutionary theory that lies at the root of transhumanist belief and secular thinking. Some scientists hold to the theory of higher air pressure and increased oxygen levels before the Flood because of the larger stature of fossil remains of plant and animals, and the high oxygen levels within amber (fossilized tree sap). It also explains the long life spans of people that has been recorded in Scripture.

---

[5] X. Figueroa, Hyperbaricstudies.com/research-studies/hyperbaric-oxygen-therapy-and-alzheimers-disease/

(An interesting article to read on this subject can be found at: https:/samaritanministries.org/blog/did-more-oxygen-and-pressure-in-the-pre-flood-world-have-health-benefit. Written on July 30th 2017 by Brian Young).

This is one example of how we can apply scripture to alleviating the problems of ill health, and how that in turn, can lead to recognition of the root problem called sin.

Once again, we are reminded of the ultimate and most important decision we must make. Will you choose Christ? Or will you choose Satan? Who or what will you put your faith in—the living Word of God, the lies of Satan, or the claims of evolution-based science and technology? In a word, who are you? Whose side are you on?

Scripture makes it clear that we cannot be both carnally and spiritually minded: 'For they that are after the flesh do mind the things of the flesh: but they that are after the Spirit, the things of the Spirit. For to be carnally minded is death; but to be spiritually minded is life and peace' (Rom.8:5–6).

# CHAPTER 7

## The Final Choice

For as in the days that were before the flood they were eating and drinking, marrying and giving in marriage, until the day that Noah entered into the ark, and knew not until the flood came, and took them all away; so shall also the coming of the Son of man be.

—Matthew 24:38–39

People have many different views about the person of Jesus Christ—what He looks like, His authority, and the extent of His involvement with mankind. Some people doubt His existence and don't believe in God at all, certainly not the Triune God of scripture. However, our very nature means we believe in something. Whether that belief is in self, science, technology, money, power, evolution, or anything else, we have a basic world view that is foundational to whatever we choose to put our faith in—in whom or what we trust.

Some Christians believe Jesus came to earth as a baby, grew to adulthood, died at Calvary, and was resurrected. This was the extent of His involvement with mankind. This is indeed a central point—the heart of scripture and the pivot of our Christian faith. However, humanity's relationship with Jesus neither begins at His entrance into the physical world of mankind, nor ends upon His return to heaven. His extent stretches from before creation to after consummation.

It is possible for believers of theistic evolution, purposely or inadvertently, to devalue the work of God in creation, which has several consequences.

Jesus in the role of Creator tends to be unacknowledged or overlooked, resulting in dispute of the absolute authority of God. This world view affects the pinnacle of creation, which is, of course, humanity, the creation of the first human beings, Adam and Eve. When God's work and God's own Word concerning the six days of creation are cast in doubt, scepticism of the continuing involvement of Christ in the affairs of mankind ensues. This can lead to confusion, particularly when belief in theistic evolution is followed by the belief in transhumanism. This state of affairs undoubtedly gives a lesser picture of the person of Christ. In this respect, the supernatural or spiritual aspects of His person are largely ignored.

Following on from this, the return of Jesus to judge mankind can also be overlooked or ignored by advocates of Christian transhumanism, who seek to speed up evolution by their own efforts. Jesus said, however:

I am Alpha and Omega, the beginning and
the end, the First and the Last. (Rev.22:13)

I am the way, the truth, and the life; no man
comes to the Father but by Me. (John 14:6)

This is the only way to heaven. Any form of evolution
or accelerated evolution has to be invalidated. The subject
of sin cannot bypass Christ either.

Some people see Jesus as forming the nation Israel, and
its status and purpose as His chosen nation. This too is
central to His plans. These intentions and their fulfilment are
well documented in scripture. His dealings with Israel reveal
many examples of how He deals with rebellious mankind.

Others see Jesus in His humanity on earth, which
is the heart of salvation. If Jesus were not fully God and
fully man, we would have no hope of salvation, no hope
of reconciliation with God the Father, and no hope of
transformation through the Holy Spirit. Had Jesus not died
on the cross as a man and risen again, our sins would not be
forgiven. This is the true Jesus.

Israel was expecting a different Jesus, one who would go
before them and lead them into physical victory over their
enemies. They were not looking for the one who would
save them from their sins. Perhaps they were looking for
a warrior leader like Alexander the Great, who overthrew
many nations but was merely mortal. He lived and died.
Israel did not see the spiritual aspect of Jesus and His
true nature. They were expecting someone else, defined
by themselves, and consequently they denied the true Son
of God.

This is a pattern that continues to repeat itself today. Christian transhumanists are treading a similar dangerous path and looking at a different Jesus. They acknowledge Him as Saviour but don't see the King of Kings and entrust themselves fully to Him. If they followed the true Jesus, there would be no need of concern for the future, as everything is totally under His Lordship. Our faith in Him is required, rather than faith in technology. Our future as citizens of His kingdom is eternally safe as long as we follow Him.[1]

The real Jesus came to His people in a way they had not anticipated—although, through God's Word, they should have foreseen it. Because they had their own human idea of who to expect, they refused to recognize Him when He came. He was opposite to what they had envisaged. 'He has no form nor comeliness; and when we shall see Him, there is no beauty that we should desire Him' (Isa.53:2).

In His physical appearance, Jesus looked like an ordinary man. He was just an average-looking man. His words and demeanour separated Him, His godly wisdom and His authority as the Voice of eternity.

His heavenly appearance is something altogether different. He is the heart and soul of scripture in its entirety. It is *this* Jesus that each one of us will meet, and *this* Jesus who will leave us with no doubt whatsoever. He is exactly the One He has claimed to be.

---

[1] Other transhumanists are following the atheist path and deny Him in every way, believing they are on their own and have to solve the problems of mankind on their own. May they recognize this untruth.

And from Jesus Christ, who is the faithful
witness, and the First Begotten of the dead,
and the Prince of the kings on earth. To
Him that loved us, and washed us from
our sins in His own blood …Behold, He
comes with clouds; and every eye shall see
Him, and they also which pierced Him;
and all kindred of the earth shall wail
because of Him. Even so Amen. "I am the
Alpha and Omega, the beginning and the
ending" says the Lord, which is, and which
was, and which is to come, the Almighty.
(Rev.1:5, 7–8)

It is *this* Jesus to whom people must give account. He
is our King over every earthly king. Whether we like it or
not, we are under His authority, which is above all other
authority. Scripture make this very clear: 'For by Him were
all things created, that are in heaven, and that are in earth,
visible and invisible, whether they be thrones, or dominions,
or principalities or powers: all things were created by Him
and for Him' (Col.1:16).

Imagine standing before Jesus and trying to explain the
transhumanist viewpoint, or why we aspired to make better
human beings than the ones He created. Imagine trying to
explain why we thought humans could make a better world
to live in than the one He lovingly and carefully prepared
for our use and enjoyment. The earth, though now marred
from its original perfection, still testifies to His handiwork.

> Because that which may be known of God
> is manifest in them; for God has showed
> it to them. For the invisible things of Him
> from the creation of the world are clearly
> seen, being understood by the things that
> are made, even His eternal power and
> Godhead; so that they are without excuse.
> (Rom.1:19–20)

I don't suppose Jesus would be impressed with transhumanist excuses, such as 'We thought that we were helping' or 'We thought we were the product of evolutionary processes'. The evidence to the contrary is far too great.

Imagine standing before Him and saying, 'We didn't believe in you. We doubted your Word.' Perhaps He would reply, 'Can you deal with your sin without Me?'That is something we can never, ever do. Even if we have the greatest technological advancements at our disposal, we can never cut ourselves free from the sin problem.

Remember, sin doesn't go away because we deny it, or because we believe it doesn't exist, or because we think that being 'good people' is enough. The reality of holiness demands total and absolute purity. This is something that not one of us has.

Think about this: you have two glasses of water in front of you. One glass contains clean, fresh water. You can only drink this pure water. You cannot drink contaminated water. But somebody has contaminated the second glass of water. You cannot drink from that glass. It must be thrown away.

This is an analogy of the holiness of God. Nothing impure can enter His kingdom. An impure heart has to be completely cleansed before it can come into His presence, and only Jesus can make us clean. Anything contaminated and impure cannot be saved. Like the second glass of water, it must be cast away. This is the judgement of God on those who have not had faith in salvation in Jesus Christ.

The atheist who does not believe in the existence of God obviously does not believe in God's judgement either. The judgement of God does not have any meaning within the world view of transhumanism. This refers to the people who are aspiring to either be or create a 'superhuman' with all knowledge and eternal life. Although they don't believe in the existence of any god, transhumanists are aspiring to become one or to create one in man's image. So, somewhere within their consciences, they are recognizing their need for God, our Triune God, but will not acknowledge it.

Yet the day of judgement is coming, and God's Word warns us to take it very seriously indeed. It will be more momentous than we can possibly imagine.

Christians attracted by transhumanism need to change course. They need to put all of their trust in Christ and not give it away to technology, which puts them in conflict with God's power and authority. No matter how good and beneficial technology is, nothing should compromise the Word of God. Technology has been given to us to help us in our life on Earth and cannot make us fit for His eternal kingdom. Not to invent a technological kingdom that is mankind's own creation.

Judgement on earth is orchestrated from the throne room of Almighty God. It is recorded for us in the book of Revelation chapter 4. Many prophetic books in the Bible talk of this, and of ensuing events concerning this judgement.

> And I saw another mighty angel come
> down from heaven, clothed with a cloud:
> and a rainbow was upon his head, and his
> face was as it were the sun, and his feet as
> pillars of fire: and he had in his hand a little
> book open: and he set his right foot upon
> the sea, and his left foot upon the earth,
> and cried with a loud voice as when a lion
> roareth. (Rev.10:1–3 KJV)

The Bible is not specific as to the identity of this angel. He appears to be very closely identified with Jesus. Scripture mentions in many places that Jesus is coming in the clouds: (Matt.26:64; Luke 21:27; Dan.7:13).The rainbow is believed to be associated with mercy in judgement. This association is first mentioned at the time of Noah, who was kept safe through the Flood, the second universal judgement of Almighty God: (Gen.9:13–14). It is seen again in the throne room of God in heaven, mentioned in Revelation 4: and again in Ezekiel 1:28.

Henry Morris, in the Henry Morris Study Bible (Green Forest AR72638: Master Books: New Leaf Publishing Group Inc), in his commentary on the passage of Revelation 10:1 *mighty angel,* says this:

> The description of this 'mighty angel'
> makes it obvious that He is none other than
> Christ Himself (compare with *1:7, 15-16.)*
> John has seen Him first as the glorified Son
> of man*(1:13),* then as God upon the throne
> *(4:10),* the Lamb with the title scroll,*(5:8),*

and the conquering Rider on the white
horse *(6:2).* Now He appears as the mighty
Angel of the Lord, claiming possession of
land and sea.

He goes on to say that the term 'little book' is from
the Greek *bibliaridion*, which is from *biblion*. The book
represents the title deed to the whole earth.

So we see that Revelation 10:1–3 could be interpreted as
a picture of the Creator claiming ownership of His creation
and, more importantly, His people. This is the one whom
proponents of transhumanism defy and deny.

The truth is that Jesus is coming soon to make war
against His enemies. He will claim back all of created order
from Satan. Jesus *is* coming back and He *will* judge all of
mankind, with no exceptions. He will not be mocked. This
is what will happen:

> And I saw heaven opened, and behold a
> white horse: and He that sat upon him
> was called Faithful and True, and in
> righteousness He does judge and make war.
> His eyes were as a flame of fire, and on
> His head were many crowns; and He had
> a name written, that no man knew but He
> Himself, and He was clothed with a vesture
> dipped in blood; and His name is called the
> Word of God. And the armies which were
> in heaven followed Him upon white horses,
> clothed in fine linen, white and clean. And
> out of His mouth goes a sharp sword, that

> with it He should smite the nations; and
> He shall rule them with a rod of iron; and
> He treads the winepress of the fierceness
> and wrath of Almighty God. And He has
> on his vesture and on His thigh, a name
> written, KING OF KINGS AND LORD
> OF LORDS. (Rev.19:11–16)

Elsewhere in the Holy Scripture, we are given a similar warning—one of many! 'Behold, the Lord comes with ten thousands of His saints. To execute judgement upon all, and to convince all that are ungodly among them of all their ungodly deeds that they have ungodly committed, and all their hard speeches which ungodly sinners have spoken against Him' (Jude 1:14–15).

We are all guilty of transgression with no exception. The difference lies with who we follow. In Christ we are forgiven. Those who follow Satan are not. This is the harsh reality. We are forgiven or not forgiven. The choice is ours.

So this is the person of Jesus Christ, whom those who have chosen to follow the secular ideals and goals promoted by Satan will meet. By putting faith in transhumanism and thereby choosing the path of human effort, those who refuse to accept salvation are taking on the Judge of all the earth. Jesus will overthrow all evil. In light of this, the goals of transhumanism, considered by many secularists to be the highest attainment of the evolutionary process, will surely fail.

This inevitable conclusion begs the question, 'Why take technology to this point?' Is it not enough to assist rather than take over?, Will we all be happier, spiritually healthier, and free from sin if we cross the line?

It is not too late to re-evaluate. Despite His wrath, God is also willing to show mercy. This door is currently open wide to those who, of their own free will, choose to repent and come to Him in faith, believing in Him and in His Word.

Biblical history gives many examples of God's mercy in judgement. Most well-known, documented, and clarified with a great deal of scientific evidence is the event of the worldwide Flood. Only Noah and his family were found to be righteous and obedient. During the Flood, they would have been totally wiped out, along with all other life, without the supernatural providence of God. It was God and God alone who sustained them during the violent upheavals of this time. If they had tried to save themselves, they would have perished, being unequal to the task. There lies a lesson for us today. We cannot save ourselves, but God can—and will, if we ask Him.

There are those who deny the Flood happened, possibly because by their denial, they can also deny the existence of judgement. Flood deniers include many avowed atheists among their number. Lyall, a famous geologist of his generation, wanted to replace the Bible record with his own ideas and persuaded many people to follow him. There are many books written on the subject of the Flood. Some are listed at the back of this book.

Satan is still plying his trade of lies and deception. It is he who is the leading motivator behind the 'accelerating evolution' ideals of transhumanism.

To give another example of how this deception works, we need look no further than the current promotion, popularity, and acceptance of neutral gender. We now have to ask: 'Are you male, female, both, or neither?' Society in past generations, following the dictates of biblical authority, adhered strictly to the man/woman relationship (Gen.2:21–25).

Dr Henry Morris puts it like this:

> The basic human institution of marriage, making 'one flesh' of husband and wife in lifelong union, is thus directly founded on the special creation of the first man and woman, for each other and for God. This would be the pattern, and norm, for all the descendants of Adam and Eve as well.[2]

Humanity has gone from this to transvestism and gender confusion. The institution of marriage has been eroded, bringing to an end the strict code of 'one woman, one man'. To embrace many partners has led to the breakdown of family units many times.

God's creation pattern has been replaced by the growing popularity of homosexuality, which is expressly forbidden and judged by God (see Rom.1:18–32). This has logically led to the normalization of same-sex marriage, which in turn has led to exogenesis.

---

[2] H. Morris, *Biblical Creationism: what each book of the Bible tells us about Creation and the Flood.* (Green Forest, AR 72638: Master Books, 2000) 25.

The word *exogenesis* was coined by J.B.S. Haldane, a scientist, back in 1924. It refers to the development of a baby outside of the mother in an artificial womb, from conception to birth. In other words, *exogenesis* means a motherless pregnancy and birth. Originally, the technique was, and to some extent still is, meant to assist with premature birth. But advocates of transhumanism have recognized its possibilities in pursuance of their own agenda. The extent to which genetic engineers have moved from God's pattern of creation is shown by the following:

> While social conservatives might be receptive about what an artificial uterus might do to the abortion paradigm, make no mistake, they'd probably not be happy that the technology also stands to make it much easier for male gay couples to have babies. All they'd need is an egg donor … The same thing goes for a transgender person wishing to have a child.[3]

The same tack is picked up in a short article published in the free newspaper *Metro*:

> We've already seen erotic cyborgs blazing a trail in the world of humanoids. Now experts believe sex robots with 'reliable artificial uteruses' could act as surrogates.

---

[3] David Warmflash, Genetic Literacy Project June 12: 2015. https://geneticliteracyproject.org/2015/06/12/artificial-wombs-the-coming-era-of-motherless-births/

The process, called exogenesis, would require a reliable artificial uterus that allows the gestation of a human being inside a machine. Dr Jordi Valiverdu says a huge amount of research has been done into robot - born humans and believes they will one day become a reality.[4]

It would be fair to suggest that the population at large is unaware of the increasing research and financial backing that is being funnelled into furthering transhumanism. Indeed, many may call it progress. Others may find it repulsive, particularly the possibility of 'robot babies'. However, the final outcome is not for us to decide.

Satan is now in the endgame, and the day of God's wrath is at hand. The deception of Satan has followed his usual strategy: doubt of God's Word and rebellion dressed as desire. Satan dangles before us something of use to mankind and, ultimately, something that puts Satan above the throne of God.

Satan's future is assured. Unbelieving people and those with doubts still have the opportunity to choose. It will be the final choice. The final choice for mankind lies, perhaps, in the not-too-distant future. It concerns the inerrant Word of God and its end-times prophecy concerning the rise of the Antichrist, the beast, and the image of the beast.(see Rev.13:1–18).

---

[4] 'Sex Robots with Artificial Uteruses', Associated Newspapers Ltd: *Metro*:Johnston Press Publishing Ltd, Portsmouth, UK, (May 6, 2017), 35.

Although there are many considerations concerning these verses, I offer a possible scenario based on the parallel agendas of Satan and transhumanism. Satan knows absolutely that God's act of creation occurred exactly as God has said in His Word. Satan knows first-hand that mankind did not evolve but was personally formed by God. Satan knows that human beings were the culmination of God's six-day creation. Satan knows that there was no death before sin, because he himself was the instigator of both sin and death. Still, Satan does not accept the authority of God over himself.

Transhumanism follows the same principle through the deceitful lies of Satan. Evolution means man in control, which means man having absolute authority. Man becomes as a god and eternal. Both agendas refuse God's sovereignty and are in open rebellion against Him. Both follow the intent of removing God from His heavenly throne and the future throne of God on the earth, which will be at Jerusalem. This is an event that scripture foretells throughout its pages. But whereas man thinks that transhumanism and its concomitant, posthumanism, will put man in control, Satan intends to help mankind achieve this goal only up to a point. He wants to be god himself. Satan will not allow transhumanist man to be a god above himself. Satan will continue to control man.

At some point, perhaps a world empire or confederation of nations will be the first to own the first truly successful transhuman, and so be in a position of power over other nations and populations. The race has likely already begun.

In scripture, the dragon, which is a name for Satan, first controls the beast and then indwells him. If or when transhumanism is achieved in its fullest sense, it would be easy to see how this 'super being' could be held in awe, amazement, and fear, leading to worship by multitudes. This being could be hailed as the saviour of mankind, the prince of peace, and the answer to all prayers, bringing the hope of an end to suffering and death.

Scripture warns us that hatred towards Christ and His followers will be intense. Satan hates Christ and all who follow him. As Christians, we are the enemy. The world will follow the beast and his image until Satan's deceit reaches its climax. All people, including his own worshippers, are to have his mark. This could be linked to transhumanism.

We are informed through scripture that the mark of the beast is the means to buy and sell. Those who refuse it will be killed.

> And he had power to give life to the image of the beast, that the image of the beast should both speak, and cause that as many as would not worship the image of the beast should be killed. And he causes all, both small and great, rich and poor, free and bond, to receive a mark in their right hand, or in their foreheads: And that no man might buy or sell, save he that had the mark, or the name of the beast, or the number of his name. Here is wisdom. Let him that has understanding count the number of the beast: for it is the number of a man; and his number is six hundred, threescore and six.(Rev.13:15–18)

Looking at the way technology is being used to further the goals of transhumanism, although those are purely speculative at this time, it would not be unreasonable to suggest that the beast and/or his image are linked to the goals of transhumanism. It is doubtful that transhumanists would deliberately embrace this, but Satan is deceiving them and using them for his own agenda.

What is currently being developed could easily be accepted, a decade or two from now, as a normal way of life. The rising dependency upon the many advances of technologies could be seen as a precursor leading towards an easy and effortless transition to the merging of man and machine.

The following scenario is taken from a Channel 4 News video that can be seen online. (June 13, 2017). It concerns interviews on the subject 'Commuters implant microchip in hand to replace train tickets'. This is under trial in Sweden on SR trains. The microchip is placed under the skin and uses the same technology as contactless and mobile payments. It can also be used for offices and bitcoin wallets. (Bitcoin is a digital currency that is growing in popularity.) The microchip can easily be updated via app and is considered more convenient than a swipe card.

This experiment can easily be seen as a major step towards a cashless society. All financial transactions could be done in this way, culminating in the eventual mark of the beast. The mark is intertwined with the worship of the beast.

So how will it affect Christians?

> If any man worship the beast and his image, and receive his mark in his forehead or in his hand, the same shall drink of the wine of the wrath of God, which is poured out without mixture into the cup of His indignation; and he shall be tormented with fire and brimstone in the presence of the holy angels and in the presence of the Lamb. And the smoke of their torment ascends up forever and ever; and they have no rest day or night, who worship the beast and his image, and who receives the mark of his name. Here is the patience of the saints; here are they that keep the commandments of God, and the faith of Jesus. (Rev.14:9–12)

Christians must not worship the beast and must not receive his mark. It is a mark of identification with the beast and submission to his authority. Once a person has that mark, there is no turning back. It will be too late for reconciliation with God and too late to repent of sin. To receive the mark or not is the final choice of mankind.

How difficult that time will be for those who already have a microchip under their skin. The microchip will make it far easier to give allegiance to him and carry his mark than to turn away and lose the right to buy and sell. Perhaps it would be better not to follow that path in the first place.

This is a dire picture of where rapid technological advancement may take us. But, as biblical history has repeatedly shown us, ultimately every plan of Satan will fail.

This last attempt of Satan to become a god over mankind is no exception. Jesus is coming back, and this is what Satan's future will be:

> And I saw an angel come down from heaven, having the key of the bottomless pit and a great chain in his hand. And he laid hold of the dragon, that old serpent, which is the Devil, and Satan, and bound him a thousand years. And cast him into the bottomless pit, and shut him up, and set a seal upon him, that he should deceive the nations no more, til the thousand years should be fulfilled; and after that he must be loosed a little season. (Rev.20:1–3)

After the thousand years, known as the millennium, comes Satan's final and absolute defeat.

> And the devil that deceived them was cast into the lake of fire and brimstone, where the beast and the false prophet are, and shall be tormented day and night forever and ever ... And death and hell were cast into the lake of fire. This is the second death. And whosoever was not found in the book of life was cast into the lake of fire. (Rev.20:10, 14–15)

So it is not a good ending for the former cherub called Lucifer, but his defeat becomes victory for those who follow Jesus Christ and put their faith in Him. We will live happily ever after. There will be no ending. Sin and death will have been defeated, and we will enjoy eternity with our Creator. We will truly be His image bearers.

That is the future. In the present, there are diverging paths one could follow. The path that begins with belief in evolution leads onward to transhumanism and is not the road to happiness. There is a line that is dangerous for advocates of technology to cross. On one side of the line, there is technology useful to man in a fallen world marred by sin. On the other side of the line, there is the desire to bypass this sinful condition by attempting to attain a godlike status. One side of the line can bring God glory in the recognition and acknowledgement of His handiwork. The other side of the line seeks to bring man glory, which will incur God's wrath.

Consequently, Christians need to avoid the prospect of being swept along by the futile promises of transhumanism. We need to resist the temptations and promises of progress, freedom, and eternal youth. These are held out to us as alternatives to God's promises, but they are false. We need to seek instead the kingdom of God.

God says to each one of us, 'See, I have set before you this day, life and good, and death and evil' (Deut.30:15).

When you make the final choice, remember the question that each one of us is required to answer.

Who *are* you?

If you are still unsure of what your response should be, please read Grace's testimony. It may help you to decide in whom to put all of your allegiance.

Please make it Christ.

# GRACE'S TESTIMONY

Grace Hope Williams bears the name Grace as a testimony to the amazing grace of God, which brought her safely into the world that He created.

Born to devout followers of our Lord Jesus Christ, Grace's growth from conception to arrival was covered by a blanket of prayer and thanksgiving. Her birth was miraculous.

Unknown to anyone but God, her umbilical cord was wrapped around her neck as she lay in the womb. Because of a complicated labour, after much deliberation, the doctors in attendance decided to administer an epidural injection to her mother. This was done in the hope of aiding a natural birth.

Although administered correctly, the epidural mysteriously did not work. A full anaesthetic and caesarean section became necessary. If the epidural injection had worked, it may well have proven fatal.

We believe that it was the mercy of the loving, Holy Father, Son, and Holy Spirit that intervened. Modern technology and skill contributed greatly to the delivery of a healthy baby, but it was by the amazing grace of God that baby Grace was born alive.

To be a child created in the image of God is a priceless part of our human existence. It far exceeds everything that technologic advancement can give us. It is unattainable by anything that transhumanism can offer us in the future. It has no potential for a relationship with our Creator God.

# RECOMMENDED READING

This is a list of books that you might like to read. Their content material covers more in depth information on the same or similar lines of *Who ARE You?* This list is in addition to book details in the footnotes:

R Hamp, *Corrupting the Image: Angels, Aliens, and the Antichrist Revealed* (Defender Publishing LLC) 2011.

G Parker, *Creation Facts of Life: How Real Science Reveals the Hand of God.* (Green Forest, AR: Master Books. (Division of New Leaf Publishing Group.) 2010.

T Horn (collaborative work), *Pandemonium's Engine: Satan's Imminent and Final Assault on the Creation of God: How the end of the Church Age, the Rise of Transhumanism, and the Coming of the Ubermensch (Overman) Herald,* (Missouri: Defender Publishing Crane) 2011.

H.M. Morris, *The Biblical Basis for Modern Science.* (Green Forest AR: Master Books. (Division of New Leaf Publishing Group) 2010.

B Hodge, *Tower of Babel: The Cultural Heritage of our Ancestors*. (Green Forest AR: Master Books. (Division of New Leaf Publishing Group) 2013.

J Free, *Trans-Human Generations: The Next Evolution of a Species*. (Mardukite Truth Seeker Press) 2012.

R Comfort, *Way of the Master*. (Alachua, FL: Bridge-Logos) 2006. Also *Scientific Facts in the Bible:100 reasons to believe the Bible is supernatural in origin* (same publisher).

Some useful websites are:
www.amazon.co.uk
www.answersingenesis.org (.uk)
www.creation.com (Creation Ministries International)
www.creationsciencemovement.com
www.genesisexpo.org.uk (creation museum – books available)
www.icr.org (Institute for Creation Research)

# ABOUT THE AUTHOR

B. M. Coaker is a committed Christian who believes firmly in the inerrant Word of God and has been a passionate creationist for many years. She has worked in the area of mental health care of the elderly for over two decades, which has provided her with much insight into brain damage and its effects. She is also a volunteer at a creationist charity. Over the years she has written articles and leaflets regarding animal welfare and creationism and has written a print-on-demand book entitled *Nature's Testimony*.

Lightning Source UK Ltd.
Milton Keynes UK
UKHW03f0314100318
319227UK00001B/6/P